www.passthetexes.com

D1402641

Pass the TExEs

Music

EC-12

Fifth Edition

FOR TEXAS TEACHERS.
A test prep manual for the TExES Music
#177 exam for grades EC-12.

by Caia McCullar BME, MM, Ph.D.
and David McCullar BME, MM

with Mark Mentze, M. Ed., M.A.

Pass the TExES Music

Fifth Edition Copyright © June 7, 2015 by Ed Publishing and Consulting
ISBN: 0-9671860-9-9

Manufactured in the United States of America

≈

Published by

Ed Publishing and Consulting
888-978-1922
E-mail: edpublishing@passthetexes.com
Website: www.passthetexes.com

Content Writers: Caia McCullar BME, MM, Ph.D. and David McCullar BME, MM
Program Designer: Mark Mentze, M.Ed., M.A.
Book/CD Designer/Program Manager: Lori Mentze
Administrative Assistant: Carla Weber

Designed using an Apple iMac™ using Adobe InDesign™. Fonts: Garamond, Bodega Sans, Matrix Tall, Helvetica Condensed, Monotype Sorts, Wingdings. PowerPoint® is a registered trademark of Microsoft® Corp.

Acknowledgments

We wish to thank all of our students, past and present, for their inspiration in making us strive to be better teachers. Their talent, energy, enthusiasm, and dedication encouraged us to constantly seek more effective ways of sharing knowledge in the teaching and learning process.

We owe a debt of gratitude to our former "master teachers" who helped us form so many of the ideas that have shaped our own teaching practices and from whom we learned so much about the art of teaching. Their commitment to our artistic and cognitive development remains with us each day and always calls us to seek a higher level in developing relationships with others and in imparting knowledge in the educational environment.

We also thank our public school and university colleagues for their advice and counsel throughout our teaching careers. Their support and encouragement have been invaluable in helping us grow as professional educators.

Finally, we wish to express appreciation to our parents for encouraging our artistry and intellect and for instilling in us a thirst for knowledge.

Contents

Preface

Dear Teachers:

This fifth edition of Pass the TExES Music EC-12 addresses the identification of standards, domains, and competencies required of music teachers for certification to teach in the public school classrooms in Texas. The focus of this manual is to provide a study guide that encourages the development of comprehensive musicianship by establishing a thorough knowledge base in all areas of music instruction at all grade levels. The material included for study is aligned with the Texas Essential Knowledge and Skills (TEKS) in music and also supports the National Standards in Music.

This manual is the result of our extensive experience in developing review courses and accompanying materials to prepare students for the state music certification examinations. Early in this process, it became apparent that there was a need to provide resources that bridge the gap between college coursework and application of this knowledge to the testing situation. The ultimate goal is to produce consummate musicians who are also highly qualified educators and life-long learners.

Please note that in the back of this manual in the Appendices you will find worksheets, the acronym memorization aid, a Competency chart, a practice test, and important contact and resource information.
.

- David and Caia McCullar

Dear Teachers:

For my certification exams, I used my graduate school study strategies. I gathered and abbreviated important information, outlined it, and created acronyms to help me memorize and recall information.

I expanded my materials in 1999 so that other teachers could benefit from my study system. Illustrations, worksheets, an interactive study module, etc., were added. The design of the Pass the TExES books provides well-organized effective review material that is easy to study and internalize. The study methods are designed to strengthen one's analysis and synthesis skills—skills necessary for success on the exam.

Since 1999 the Pass the ExCET and now Pass the TExES series of test prep books has helped hundreds of teachers prepare effectively and efficiently for Texas teacher certification exams.

Please contact edpublishing@passthetexes.com should you have any questions during your study time, and please let us know how you did on the test!

- Mark Mentze

Introduction

WHAT IS THE TEXES?

TExES stands for the Texas Examinations of Educator Standards. Legislation was passed in 1981 that mandates all public elementary and secondary teachers be tested and pass at least two certification tests. This book covers one of the two—the other exam is the Pedagogy and Professional Responsibilities (PPR). Ed Publishing also publishes Pass the TExES PPR.

WHERE CAN I REGISTER FOR THE TEXES

Registration information is found at www.texes.ets.org. Important contact information:

TExES Program for Texas Teachers
Educational Testing Service
www.texes.ets.org

or the SBEC (State Board for Teacher Certification):

SBEC/TEA
1701 North Congress Ave.
WBT 5-100
Austin, TX 78701-1494
Phone: 888-863-5880 or
(512) 463-9734
www.tea.state.tx.us

CHARACTERISTICS OF THE EXAM

The TExES program is designed to assess subject matter knowledge and professional knowledge required of an entry-level educator in Texas public schools. All the exams in the TExES program are criterion referenced; that is, they are designed to measure your knowledge in relation to an established competence (criterion) rather than in relation to the performance of other candidates.

HOW SHOULD I STUDY FOR THE EXAM?

Of course you should obtain the study manual provided by ETS/SBEC (see www.texes.ets. org). In the back of that manual several reference books are listed which would be helpful to review if you have quite a bit of time or have been out of college for some time. They will likely be available at your local university or community college library. However, time is most likely limited,
so we encourage you to use this book in conjunction with the study manual provided by the ETS/SBEC and you will have a complete test preparation package. Other publishers have produced TExES study manuals and they may have written additional sample test questions that could be useful, but use our study approach and keep in mind that their questions may or may not be on the actual test. We encourage you to follow the Steps for Success in this manual and do as many exercises and assignments as you have time for.

WHEN ARE THE EXAMS GIVEN AND HOW MUCH DO THEY COST?

All the information you need regarding test dates, site locations, fees, registration procedures, and policies can be found at www.texes.ets.org, where you can also register online.

Introduction, cont'd.

EXPLAIN THE PASS THE TEXES PROGRAM...WHY DO I NEED IT?

This study program is designed in such a way to make preparing for the exam more efficient for the learner, and more effective. The program is all about TOOLS...we give you several tools which will help you prepare for the exam like no other program. The exercises presented in our program encourage methods of study that will help you retain more information in a shorter amount of time. The program exercises were designed to naturally strengthen the analysis and synthesis skills of the learner, which is key when choosing the best answers to the test questions. Our program addresses several learning styles and preferences.

WHAT ARE THE FEATURES OF THE PROGRAM?

Of course it is essential to be knowledgeable about the subject matter, but these tests consist of many subjective questions. The following features will help you organize the content information. The **Acronym Exercise** in Appendix I is designed to help you recall the **Competency Key Titles** (see Competency 1's **Key Title** at the top of p. 14-15); the **Key Titles** are designed to recall the **Competency** content, and with the help of the **Key Words** (see p. 14), the content for each Competency should be recalled more efficiently.

The official ETS/SBEC TExES study manual contains lettered descriptive statements for each Competency. The **Key Descriptor** exercise described in the Steps for Success, p. 10, (and in each Competency study section) asks you to condense these descriptive statements into short phrases which require you to *analyze and synthesize* the ETS/SBEC descriptive statements instead of just passively reading them. They are actually difficult to study as they are written in academic language, long sentences, and include content in parentheses.

The **Worksheets** in Appendix I are very important, and help you understand the framework of the material. You may copy these pages and complete them a few times to test your recall. The **Practice Test Method** explained in Appendix I will help you choose the BEST answer to the exam questions. There is also a **Practice Test Worksheet** and **Practice Questions** in Appendix III in this manual. Please follow the directions on the Practice Test Method page in Appendix I to answer these questions and any other practice test questions available from various sources.

The **PowerPoint® Interactive Study Module** is the icing on the cake. The module is a unique way to study the framework of the content. It breaks down the Competency definitions into phrasing for better understanding. See instructions for use on the last page in this manual.

TWO KEYS TO THIS PROGRAM

#1   **UNDERSTANDING IMPORTANT CONCEPTS FOR EACH COMPETENCY.**

#2   **CONNECTING TEST QUESTIONS TO THE CORRECT COMPETENCY AND CHOOSING THE ANSWER, KEEPING IN MIND THE SBEC POINT OF VIEW.**

GOOD LUCK! After you receive your scores, send your success stories and comments to edpublishing@passthetexes.com. We would love to hear from you. Visit www.passthetexes.com and read the many testimonials we have received about the program.

Steps for Success

NOTE: It is recommended that 3-4 weeks is allowed to complete this study program process. There are certain exercises that you may not have time for. However, choose the parts of the program that you feel you can realistically accomplish, set some goals, and plot them on a calendar.

1. STEP ONE (ACTIVE STUDY)

To begin your test preparation you will need the ETS/SBEC official study manual. The study manual is available online at www.texes.ets.org, and the study material from the manual is included in our manual in Appendix III; the entire manual is included with our supplementary files. If you feel you need additional study, there are recommended resources listed in the back of the ETS/SBEC manual. We call the lettered study information in the ETS/SBEC manual "Descriptors". This is key conceptual information, although the statements are sometimes difficult to understand and study because of their length and wordiness. The authors' study material in this manual is an *expansion* of these Descriptors. Our "Descriptor Exercise" below will help you understand the Competency concepts more clearly.

"Active Study" Instructions:

- **Review:** Review the study content for the first Competency in this manual. Study the Key Title, Descriptor Highlights, and Key Words. Use your highlighter to highlight key information, and use the Internet to quickly look up information you need further clarification about and write additional notes in the margins.
- **Descriptor Exercise:** *Use the official ETS/SBEC study material in the back of this book for this exercise.* Before you move on to Competency 2, do the Descriptor Exercise for Competency 1. This exercise is a great tool to help you understand what the SBEC wants you to know, and will help you retain that information more efficiently and more effectively. This exercise will require you to study and analyze the lettered descriptive statements under each Competency definition in the ETS/SBEC manual (not just passively read them), and synthesize them down to a phrase that is meaningful to you and that will concisely sum up what the statement is conveying. (See the example at left.) Look at page 14 of this manual. On the blanks provided you will paraphrase the lettered descriptors from the official ETS/SBEC manual. Keep your phrase at <u>five words or less</u>; put one phrase on each blank. For the first descriptor, write your phrase on the first blank. For the second descriptor, write that on the second blank, and so on. It is helpful to letter your blanks just like the descriptors are lettered in the official study manual. Then transfer all of your phrases to Worksheet 4 in Appendix I of this manual for easier study. You can carry Worksheet 4 with you during the day for quick reference as well.

> **EXAMPLE:**
> "Knows the typical stages of cognitive, social, physical, and emotional development of students in early childhood through grade 12." The paraphrase for this bullet point is "<u>stages of development</u>" Taken from bullet 1, Comp. 1, PPR EC-12

2. STEP TWO (MEMORIZATION and RECALL)

The Descriptor Exercise is designed to not only help you understand with the SBEC wants you to know, but helps you commit information to memory. When you read your phrases, you will hopefully be able to recall additional details...thus exercising your ability to recall information. In the example at left, the important information that we left out was the *stages of development*: "cognitive, social, physical, and emotional". This is what you will hopefully recall when you read the phrase "stages of development". A good way to study with Worksheet 4 is to put it beside the SBEC study material and go back and forth, checking your recall of additional details about the Competency concepts.

Do Worksheets 1-5 and do the Acronym Exercise in Appendix I. The goal is to organize and internalize the framework of the material for better recall. Use the PowerPoint® study module to assist you in understanding the Competency definitions. One of the assignments on Worksheet 5 asks you to write down everything you can recall about each Competency—this is a great exercise to check "what you know and what you don't know."

 WE RECOMMEND: On the test booklet before the test write down your full acronym or at least the acronym for the Domains you are weakest in (see Appendix I), then your Key Titles. As you answer each question, if needed, refer to this Competency framework to refresh your memory.

Steps for Success, cont'd.

STEP THREE (ASSESSMENT)

Answer the practice test questions provided in this manual in Appendix III, and any practice test questions you have access to, using our **Practice Test Method** (described in Appendix I). The seven italicized questions you see on our Practice Test Worksheet in Appendix III represent a very methodical thought process we recommend using during your preparation. By following this method carefully while working each question, you will better connect the test question to the Competencies which is key to choosing the best answer, and you will understand the point of view of the SBEC, which is very important to your success. This process will give you legitimate reasons for choosing answers, which will guide you on the actual test. Choosing correct answers based on incorrect reasoning only sets you up for failure. In the seventh step of this process, you are analyzing for yourself why the test writers chose the answers they did, and that is KEY, especially on the more subjective questions. Doing this important analysis will help you understand the philosophy of the test writers, as well as strengthen your analysis skills...skills that you will need on the actual test.

THE OVERALL APPROACH

The overall approach you are following when using the Pass the TExES study program of study is in two parts:

Part One: Knowledge and Comprehension

Part Two: Critical Thinking Skill Development

According to Bloom's Taxonomy knowledge and comprehension material must be mastered before one can apply these concepts in the test questions. The Pass the TExES program encourages the development of higher level thought processes such as application, evaluation, and analysis and synthesis...processes Bloom's Taxonomy categorizes at the top end of learning. The exercises we employ are designed to exercise and increase these higher-level thought processes, thus allowing for greater success on the exam. That is why this method includes both lower level memorization activities and then moves into exercises using the higher level thought processes. The goal, of course, is to know this material well and be able to analyze test questions and choose correct answers on the test.

 This program has made all the difference for many teachers since 1999. Read testimonials and purchase additional copies of this book and other books at www.passthetexes.com. Seminars may be available to the general public and they are always available for Texas colleges and universities, school districts, Alternative Certification Programs, and Education Service Centers.

NOTE: By carefully following this program of study we feel that you will be well-prepared for your TExES exam. However, we do not guarantee a passing grade on the exam. We encourage you to contact us during your study time should you have any questions. If you purchase a book and decide you cannot use it, please contact us right away, and return it within seven days of receipt to receive a refund. We are sorry, but ebooks are not returnable.

Domain I:

Listening

Competencies 1-3

(25% of the test)

Music EC-12 Standard I:

The music teacher has a comprehensive visual and aural knowledge of musical perception and performance.

Music EC-12 Standard III:

The music teacher has a comprehensive knowledge of music notation.

Music EC-12 Standard V:

The music teacher has a comprehensive knowledge of music history and the relationship of music to history, society, and culture.

Music EC-12 Standard VI:

The music teacher applies a comprehensive knowledge of music to evaluate musical compositions, performances, and experiences.

13

I. Elements

Key Descriptors:

_____

_____

_____

_____

_____

_____

_____

_____

_____

_____

_____

_____

_____

_____

_____

_____

_____

NOTE: Refer to the bullet points under each Competency in the ETS/SBEC study guide. Analyze each bullet point, and synthesize it down to a paraphrase that is meaningful to you, using no more than 5 words. List those phrases in order on the lines above. It may help to number the bullet points and the lines above. When complete,

Key Words:

Music Symbols and Terms

Melodic and Harmonic Intervals

Scales and Pitch Collections

Rhythm and Meter

Dynamics and Form

Texture and Timbre

Aural Analysis of Musical Works

Rhythm

DESCRIPTOR HIGHLIGHTS

- Recognizes and interprets music symbols and terms aurally.
- Identifies melodic and harmonic intervals.
- Recognizes scales and pitch collections.
- Identifies and interprets rhythmic and melodic concepts aurally.

- Describes melodic, harmonic, and textural aspects of a musical composition.
- Analyzes chordal structures, harmonic progressions, cadences, and textures.

1. Elements

Competency 1:

The teacher applies standard terminology to describe and analyze various elements in a musical recording.

Aural skills development is one of the most important resources used by the music teacher in the classroom on a daily basis. The ability to aurally recognize and describe aspects of a musical composition or performance is a necessary requirement for comprehensive musicianship.

The prospective music teacher must show evidence of a thorough knowledge base of musical styles from the whole of music history. In addition, the music teacher must have a keenly developed ear in order to diagnose problems and prescribe effective solutions related to student performance.

A. **MELODY** - a succession of single pitches
- Intervals - the distance between two different pitches
- Scales - the orderly graduated arrangement of ascending or descending pitches
- Pitch Collections - the use of something other than complete scales from which a melody or composition is derived

B. **RHYTHM** - the organization of music over time using long and short note and rest values
- Meter - a systematic grouping of beats and their divisions in regularly recurring patterns
- Syncopation - the disruption of the normal accent in a measure by shifting it to an unexpected beat
- Augmentation - the proportional enlargement of rhythmic values
- Diminution - the proportional reduction of rhythmic values
- Hemiola - a rhythmic device found in all periods of Western music; alternation of triple meter at two different metrical levels, as in juxtaposition of 6/8 and 3/4

C. **TEXTURE** - the horizontal and vertical relationship of musical elements
- Monophonic - music composed for a single unaccompanied voice or unison choir
- Homophonic - music in which the parts move more or less together (chordal), or in which one prominent melody is given a chordal accompaniment
- Polyphonic - music with more than one voice part
- Chord Structures - combinations of concurrently sounding or arpeggiated notes, the identity of which is understood and named without accounting for any foreground elaboration (i.e., suspensions, appoggiaturas, passing tones, auxiliary tones, etc.)
- Chord Progressions - successions of functional chords proceeding by strong root movements which may be elaborated by intervening non-functional chords (auxiliary chord, passing chord, appoggiatura chord)
- Cadences - a closing pattern or formula that terminates a phrase, section, or complete composition

D. **TIMBRE** - tone color or quality: Vocal, Instrumental, Keyboard, Synthesized Sound

E. **DYNAMICS** - varying degrees of loud and soft
- Terraced Dynamics - expressive style typical of some early music, particularly Baroque, in which volume levels shift abruptly from soft to loud and back without gradual crescendos and decrescendos
- Crescendo/Decrescendo

F. **FORM** - the organization and structure of a composition
- Binary - a 2-part form
- Ternary - a 3-part form
- Twelve Bar Blues - a I, IV, V chord progression, often used in jazz style, making use primarily of dominant 7th chords played over twelve bars or measures
- Rondo - a repeated return of musical material in phrases and sections interspersed with phrases and sections of new musical material (ABACADA, etc.)
- Theme and Variations - a style of composition that first presents a basic theme and then develops and alters that theme in successive statements
- Sonata Allegro - a multi-sectional form often used as a first-movement form
- Fugue - a polyphonic procedure involving a specified number of voices in which a motive (subject) is exposed, in each voice, in an initial tonic/dominant relationship, then developed by contrapuntal means

G. **SYMBOLS AND TERMS** - interpretive and performance markings on a musical score
- Tempo Markings
- Embellishments
- Dynamic Markings
- Articulations

2. Styles and Genres

Key Descriptors:

_____

_____

_____

_____

_____

_____

_____

_____

_____

_____

_____

_____

_____

_____

_____

_____

_____

NOTE: Refer to the bullet points under each Competency in the ETS/SBEC study guide. Analyze each bullet point, and synthesize it down to a paraphrase that is meaningful to you, using no more than 5 words. List those phrases in order on the lines above. It may help to number the bullet points and the lines above. When complete,

Key Words:

Western Influence
> Middle Ages
> Renaissance
> Baroque
> Classical
> Romantic
> Modern (20th - 21st Cen.)

Non-Western Music

U.S. Musical Heritage

Texas Musical Heritage

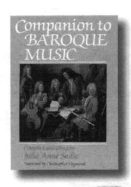

D E S C R I P T O R   H I G H L I G H T S

- Identifies musical styles, characteristics, works, and composers of Middle Ages, Renaissance, Baroque, Classical, Romantic, and Modern music in a recorded example.
- Characterizes and classifies examples of Non-Western music (Indonesian gamelan, African drumming, Indian raga, Cuban salsa) by genre,

style, culture, and historical period in a recorded example.
- Recognizes and describes music that reflects United States and Texas heritage (folk songs, work songs, jazz, blues, gospel, Tejano, country, bluegrass) in a recorded example

2. Styles and Genres

Competency 2:

The teacher recognizes and describes music of diverse genres, styles, and cultures in a musical recording.

A. TYPES OF COMPOSITIONS

- Middle Ages (c. 500-1400)
  Plainchant, Organum, Mass, Isorhythmic motet, Secular songs, Instrumental Dances

- Renaissance (1400-1600)
  Ordinary of the Mass (polyphonic settings), Motet, Chanson, Madrigal, Instrumental Dances, Instrumental Pieces

- Baroque (1600-1750)
  Motet (with instrumental accompaniment), Mass (with instrumental accompaniment), Opera, Cantata, Oratorio, Sonata, Concerto, Fugue, Suite

- Classical (c. 1750-c. 1820)
  Mass, Opera, Oratorio, Solo Concerto, String Quartet, Symphony

- Romantic (c. 1820-1900)
  Opera, Oratorio, Art Song and Song Cycle, Character pieces (piano), Sonata, String Quartet, Symphony, Symphonic Poem (Tone Poem)

- 20th Century Trends (1900-2000)
  Nationalism, Impressionism, Expressionism, Neoclassicism, Musique Concrete (Electronic Music), Aleatory (Chance) Music, Minimalism

- Non-Western Music
  Indonesian Gamelan, African Drumming, Indian Raga, Cuban Salsa, Asian Influence

- United States Musical Heritage
  Folk Songs, Work Songs, Gospel, Spirituals, Ragtime, Blues, Jazz, Country, Bluegrass, Rhythm and Blues, Rock and Roll, Barbershop Quartet, Musical Theatre

- Texas Musical Heritage
  Singing Cowboys and Range Songs, Tejano, Mariachi

3. Evaluation

Key Descriptors:

_____
_____
_____
_____
_____
_____
_____
_____
_____
_____
_____
_____
_____
_____
_____
_____

NOTE: Refer to the bullet points under each Competency in the ETS/SBEC study guide. Analyze each bullet point, and synthesize it down to a paraphrase that is meaningful to you, using no more than 5 words. List those phrases in order on the lines above. It may help to number the bullet points and the lines above. When complete,

Key Words:

Rhythmic Error Detection

Melodic Error Detection

Timbre Recognition

Texture Recognition

Form Recognition

Stylistic and Expressive Qualities

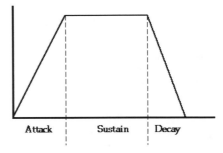

Attack Sustain Decay

D E S C R I P T O R   H I G H L I G H T S

- Identifies vocal, instrumental, and keyboard sounds
- Recognizes and distinguishes various timbres
- Recognizes accurate rhythm, pitch, intonation, and tone quality
- Recognizes and diagnoses performance problems
- Detects rhythmic and melodic errors accurately

- Identifies and analyzes musical forms in performance
- Identifies and analyzes stylistic and expressive characteristics in musical performance

3. Evaluation

Competency 3:

The teacher evaluates and critiques musical compositions and performances in a musical recording.

A. COMPOSITIONAL TYPE

- Is the composition vocal, instrumental, or keyboard?
  Example: Vocal - one or more voices
  Instrumental - one or more instruments
  Keyboard - piano, harpsichord, organ, synthesizer
- What type of composition is heard?
  Example: symphony, opera, oratorio, art song, character piece (piano), string quartet, madrigal, motet, Mass, other forms

B. COMPOSITIONAL TEXTURE

- How many voices/instruments are heard?
  Example: Solo, Duet, Trio, Quartet, Quintet, Octet, small ensemble, large ensemble
- What type(s) of voices/instruments are heard?
  Example: Vocal-Soprano, Mezzo Soprano, Alto, Tenor, Baritone, Bass
  Instrumental - Strings, Woodwind, Brass, Percussion
  Elementary Classroom - Recorders, Orff Instruments, Autoharp, Assorted Rhythm Instruments
  Keyboard - Piano, Organ, Harpsichord, Synthesizer
- How are voices/instruments grouped?
  Example: Vocal-Unison, SA, SSA, SSAA, TB, TTB, TTBB, SAB, SATB, SSAATTBB
  Strings - number of violins, violas, cellos, double basses
  Band - balance and use of woodwinds, brass, and percussion
  Concerto - solo instrument and full orchestra accompaniment
  Opera and Oratorio - solo singers (recitative and aria), small ensembles, full chorus

- Is the composition accompanied or unaccompanied? If accompanied, what types of instruments are used? *Example:* Keyboard, Basso Continuo, Guitar, Harp, Banjo, other combinations of instruments

C. COMPOSITIONAL ELEMENTS

- What is the rhythmic basis of the composition? *Example:* simple, compound, duple, triple, mixed meter, polyrhythms
- What is the tonal concept used in the composition? *Example:* major, minor, modal, pentatonic, atonal, bitonal, polytonal
- What probable formal structure is used to organize the composition? *Example:* Binary, Ternary, 12 Bar Blues, Rondo, Theme and Variations, Sonata Allegro, Fugue

D. COMPOSITIONAL CONTEXT

- If there is a text, what language is heard? *Example:* Latin, Italian, German, French, Spanish, English
- What cultural influences are present in the composition? *Example:* traditional, non-traditional, Western, Non-Western, or other cultural influences used by the composer in creating a musical work

Domain II:

Music Theory and Composition

Competencies 4-5

(17% of the test)

Music EC-12 Standard I:

The music teacher has a comprehensive visual and aural
knowledge of musical perception and performance.

Music EC-12 Standard III:

The music teacher has a comprehensive knowledge of music notation.

Music EC-12 Standard IV:

The music teacher creates and arranges music.

Music EC-12 Standard VI:

The music teacher applies a comprehensive knowledge of music to
evaluate musical compositions, performances, and experiences.

4. __Notation__

Key Descriptors:

_____

_____

_____

_____

_____

_____

_____

_____

_____

_____

_____

_____

NOTE: Refer to the bullet points under each Competency in the ETS/SBEC study guide. Analyze each bullet point, and synthesize it down to a paraphrase that is meaningful to you, using no more than 5 words. List those phrases in order on the lines above. It may help to number the bullet points and the lines above. When complete,

Key Words:

Music Symbols and Terms

Rhythm and Meter

Staff, Clefs and Key Signatures

Scales and Pitch Collections

Melodic and Harmonic Intervals

Tonalities

Chord Structures

Harmonic Progressions

Cadences

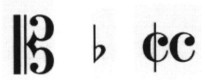

Time signature and

Example of "meter"

authentic cadence

V - I

D E S C R I P T O R   H I G H L I G H T S

- Understands interpretive symbols and terms, such as dynamics, embellishments, articulation markings, tempo markings.
- Understands the elements of rhythm and meter.
- Applies knowledge of the staff, clefs, keys, scales, and pitch collections.
- Identifies melodic and harmonic intervals.

- Understands chordal structures and harmonic progressions.
- Understands the types, characteristics, and uses of cadences.
- Describes the rhythm, melody, harmony, and formal structure of a musical work

4. Notation

Competency 4:

The teacher knows how to read, write, and interpret standard music notation.

Understanding and interpreting elements of the musical score is a basic skill needed by all musicians. The symbols on a musical page represent the intentions of the composer or arranger for the ultimate performance product. The ability to visually recognize and accurately reproduce aspects of a musical composition is a necessary requirement for comprehensive musicianship.

A. INTERPRETIVE AND PERFORMANCE TERMINOLOGY
- Dynamics - varying degrees of loud and soft: Pianissimo, Piano, Mezzo Piano, Mezzo Forte, Forte, Fortissimo, Crescendo, Decrescendo, Sforzando
- Embellishments - musical ornamentations: Ornaments, Auxiliary Tones (Non-Harmonic Tones)
- Articulation Markings - characteristics of attack and delay of single tones or groups of tones and the means by which these are produced: Staccato, Legato, Phrasing, Bowing, Tonguing, etc.
- Tempo Markings - terms used to indicate the speed of a composition or section of a composition: Largo, Lento, Adagio, Andante, Moderato, Allegretto, Allegro, Presto, Prestissimo, Ritardando, Accelerando, Rubato

B. RHYTHMIC AND METRICAL COMPONENTS
- Beat - the temporal unit of a composition
- Tempo - the speed of a composition or section of a composition
- Simple Meter - meters multiplied by two
- Compound Meter - meters multiplied by three
- Note and Rest Values - varying lengths of sound and silence in a musical composition
- Conducting Patterns - the indication of the metric pulse through the conductor's right hand and interpretive cues from the left hand

C. MELODIC COMPONENTS
- Staff - a series of five horizontal lines on and between which musical notes and rests are written
- Clefs - a sign given at the beginning of a staff to indicate the pitch and notes (treble, bass, alto, tenor, etc.)
- Musical Alphabet - the letter names used to indicate pitches
- Key Signatures - sharps or flats shown at the beginning of each staff to indicate the key of a composition
- Scales - the underlying tonal material of a composition

arranged in the order of rising pitches (major, minor - three forms, modal, gypsy, pentatonic, whole tone, chromatic, twelve tone, blues)

D. INTERVALS - THE DISTANCE OR DIFFERENCE BETWEEN TWO PITCHES
- Major (2nds, 3rds, 6ths, 7ths)
- Minor (2nds, 3rds, 6ths, 7ths)
- Augmented - one half step larger than a perfect or major interval
- Diminished - one half step smaller than a perfect or minor interval
- Perfect (4th, 5th, Octave)
- Enharmonic Spellings - tones that are the same scale degree of the chromatic scale but which are named and written differently

E. VERTICAL SONORITY - Three or more tones sounded simultaneously; two simultaneous tones are usually designated as an interval (see above)
- Major Chords; Minor Chords; Augmented Chords; Diminished Chords; 7th; 9th; Augmented 6th Chords (Italian, French, German); Neopolitan Chord; Harmonic chord progressions

F. CADENCES - A melodic or harmonic formula that occurs at the end of a composition, a section, or a phrase, conveying the impression of a momentary or permanent conclusion
- Authentic; Plagal; Deceptive; Half

G. HARMONIC TEXTURES
- Monophonic; Homophonic; Polyphonic

H. DESCRIPTIVE CHARACTERISTICS
- Modal; Tonal; Atonal; Ostinato; Doublings; Melody; Countermelody

5. Composition

Key Descriptors:

_____

_____

_____

_____

_____

_____

_____

_____

_____

_____

_____

_____

_____

_____

_____

NOTE: Refer to the bullet points under each Competency in the ETS/SBEC study guide. Analyze each bullet point, and synthesize it down to a paraphrase that is meaningful to you, using no more than 5 words. List those phrases in order on the lines above. It may help to number the bullet points and the lines above. When complete,

Key Words:

Scoring Techniques

Transpositions

Formal Structures

Arranging

Improvisation

Evaluating Musical Works

Critiquing Musical Works

Rhythmic Augmentation: the note values of the motive are doubled.

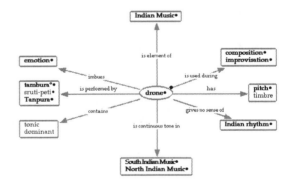

D E S C R I P T O R   H I G H L I G H T S

- Understands techniques of composition and arranging of vocal and instrumental music.
- Applies knowledge of musical forms.
- Analyzes compositional devices.
- Understands how to improvise melodically, rhythmically, and harmonically.

- Evaluates and critiques musical selections effectively.
- Uses appropriate terminology to evaluate stylistic characteristics of a musical work.
- Offers constructive diagnostic and prescriptive suggestions for improving a musical composition.

5. Composition

Competency 5:

The teacher understands methods and techniques of musical composition and improvisation and knows how to arrange music for specific purposes and settings.

A. MUSICAL FORMS - **organization and structure of a music composition**

- Binary, Ternary, Rondo, Sonata Allegro, Theme and Variations, Fugue, Concerto, Opera, 12 Bar Blues, Strophic and Through Composed (Poetic/Musical Forms)

B. COMPOSITIONAL DEVICES - **techniques used in the construction of musical works**

- Repetition/Contrast, Delayed Resolution, Augmentation/Diminution, Ostinato, Fugue, Tone Row

C. COMPOSING AND ARRANGING (VOICES AND INSTRUMENTS) - the practice of creating new musical settings from original ideas; the practice of putting preexisting musical material into a different setting

- Scoring Techniques (including technology applications), Transpositions of Instruments, Ranges and Tessituras for Voices and Instruments, Setting Text to Music (syllabic stress)

D. IMPROVISATION TECHNIQUES - methods used to perform music spontaneously with out the aid of written music or memory; also, the art of introducing improvised material into a written composition

- Question and Answer, Drone, Ostinato, Vocal Jazz Techniques (scat syllables, etc.), Instrumental Jazz Techniques, Improvised Movement Techniques, Improvised Accompaniments for Stated Melodies

E. EVALUATING AND CRITIQUING MUSICAL COMPOSITIONS - strategies for careful ly appraising the qualitative and quantitative aspects of a musical work

- Stylistic Description, Appropriate Terminology, Formal Structure, Compositional Materials and Techniques

Domain III:
Music History and Culture

Competencies 6-7

(17% of the test)

Music EC-12 Standard V:
The music teacher has a comprehensive knowledge of music history and the relationship of music to history, society, and culture.

6. Western Music

Key Descriptors:

_____

_____

_____

_____

_____

_____

_____

_____

_____

_____

_____

_____

_____

_____

_____

NOTE: Refer to the bullet points under each Competency in the ETS/SBEC study guide. Analyze each bullet point, and synthesize it down to a paraphrase that is meaningful to you, using no more than 5 words. List those phrases in order on the lines above. It may help to number the bullet points and the lines above. When complete,

Key Words:

Middle Ages

Renaissance

Baroque

Classical

Romantic

Modern

D E S C R I P T O R   H I G H L I G H T S

- Recognizes major periods, styles, and individuals in the history of Western music.
- Describes the characteristics of major periods and styles in the history of Western music.
- Understands the significance of composers and other contributors to the history of Western music.
- Analyzes and classifies examples of Western music by genre, style, culture, or historical period.

- Understands the important historical, social, artistic, and cultural events impacting the development of Western music.
- Recognizes and comprehends the chronological links among major periods and musical styles in the development of Western music.
- Links Western musical compositions and their composers using stylistic characteristics, traits, and techniques.

6. Western Music

Competency 6:

The teacher demonstrates a comprehensive knowledge of the history of Western music.

A strong understanding of the history of music from its earliest beginning to the present day provides a basis for musical comprehension. The Texas Essential Knowledge and Skills (TEKS), on which schools must base their music curriculum, devotes an entire strand to the "Historical and Cultural Heritage" of music.

Knowledge of the composers, genres, styles, and cultural influences of each era of music history forms the foundation for analyzing and interpreting the musical score. A working knowledge and understanding of the historical aspects of music impacts the teacher from both a theoretical and performance practice perspective.

A. MIDDLE AGES MUSIC (C. 500-1400)

- Moves in free chant rhythm; beat groupings of threes (13th century); beat groupings of twos (14th century)
- Stepwise, melodic movement; limited vocal ranges; use of the church modes
- Monophonic; polyphony for 2-4 voices; consonant intervals (unisons, 4ths, 5ths, and octaves)
- Plainchant; organum; songs with verses; hymns; free and fixed poetic forms in secular music
- Small choirs (monophonic chant); soloists (polyphonic music); instrumental music (generally improvised)
- 13th century known as the Ars Antiqua; 14th century known as the Ars Nova
- Types of compositions include: Mass; plainchant settings of parts of Mass; isorhythmic motet; secular songs; instrumental dances (estampie)
- Significant composers include: Pope Gregory; Leonin; Perotin; de Vitry; Machaut; Landini; Dunstable; Dufay

B. RENAISSANCE MUSIC (1400-1600)

- Beat groupings of twos; more complex rhythms; some syncopation
- Moves mostly in steps; expanded vocal ranges
- Use of imitation (points of imitation); 4 parts; dissonance at the cadence points; text painting
- Fixed poetic forms replaced by imitation; songs with verses; hymns
- Homophony; polyphony; 5 or more voices in the 16th century; music for specific instruments
- Types of compositions include: Polyphonic settings of parts of the Mass; motet; madrigal; secular songs; instrumental pieces
- Significant composers include: Josquin des Prez; Palestrina; Vittoria; the Gabrielis; Gesualdo; Monteverdi; Tallis; Morley

Continued

6. Western Music, cont'd.

C. BAROQUE MUSIC (1600-1750)
- Free (recitative); steady, clear meters
- Moves in steps and skips; use of countrapuntal techniques; sequencing; use of ornamentation
- Major and minor scales; polyphony; homophony
- Equal-tempered tuning (replaced mean-tone); terrace dynamics
- Forms include: AB; ABA; fugue; development of multi-movement compositions
- Small choral groups; soloists; small orchestras (strings, winds, continuo)
- Types of compositions include: Mass and motet with instrumental accompaniment; opera; oratorio; cantata; sonata; concerto; fugue; suite
- Significant composers include: Schutz; Frescobaldi; Lully; Buxtehude; Corelli; Purcell; Vivaldi; Rameau; J. S. Bach; Handel; Domenico Scarlatti

D. CLASSICAL MUSIC (C.1750-C.1820)
- Free (recitative); clearly defined meters; rhythmic variety
- Thematic (motivic) in nature; 8 bar phrase structure
- Major-minor tonality; use of modulation; change of key within a movement; use of principal triads (primarily triadic chord structures)
- Sonata-Allegro; rondo; theme and variations; multi-movement compositions
- Absolute music with no extramusical association most common
- Instruments more prominent than the voice; larger orchestras without use of continuo
- Types of compositions include: Mass; opera; oratorio; unaccompanied sonata; symphony; concerto; string quartet
- Significant composers include: Gluck; C.P.E. Bach; Billings; Haydn; Mozart; Beethoven

E. ROMANTIC MUSIC (C.1820-1900)
- Variety of meters; variety of rhythmic patterns; meter changes within movements
- Lyrical; longer phrases; phrases less regular
- Major-minor tonality; expanded use of modulation and chromaticism; counterpoint; greater use of dissonance; 7th and 9th chords more prominent
- Wider range of dynamic levels
- Classical forms are expanded; multi-movement works; miniatures (character piece for piano, art song for voice); symphonic poem (programmatic)
- Growth of orchestra; large choruses; solo voice and piano; opera
- Types of compositions include: Solo song cycle; character pieces; symphonic poem (tone poem); symphony; string quartet; opera; oratorio; Requiem Mass
- Significant composers include: Schubert, Schumann, Brahms, Wolf, Berlioz, Liszt; Mendelssohn; Chopin; Rossini; Donizetti; Bellini; Wagner; Verdi; Puccini; Saint-Saens; Tchaikovsky; Mussorgsky; Rimsky-Korsakov; Strauss; Mahler

6. Western Music, cont'd.

F. MODERN MUSIC (1900-PRESENT)

- Shifting meters; asymmetrical meters; non-metric; multi-metric; displaced barline; primitivism
- Extreme chromaticism; twelve-tone technique; angularity of melodic structure; dissonant leaps; disjunct progressions
- Breakdown of tonality; harsh dissonance; atonality; polytonality; new methods of tonal structure; use of 9th, 11th, 13th chords; neo-modality; open chord structures; parallelism; whole-tone mode; less prominence of barline regularity; wide spacing; extreme registers
- Neoclassicism (used older forms from Renaissance and Baroque while using 20th century rhythms, melodies, harmonies, timbres); freer forms were developed
- Emphasis on percussive sounds; synthesized sounds; extreme ranges and colors
- Types of compositions: Impressionism; Expressionism; Aleatory music; Musique concrete; Minimalism
- Significant composers include: Debussy; Ravel; Schoenberg; Ives; Stravinsky; Bartok; Kodaly; Orff; Barber; Copland; Britten; Berg; Webern; Gershwin; Joplin; Ellington; Bernstein; Poulenc; Messiaen; Boulez; Xenakis; Varese; Stockhausen; Chavez; Villa-Lobos; Cage; Glass

7. Culture and Music

Key Descriptors:

_____

_____

_____

_____

_____

_____

_____

_____

_____

_____

_____

_____

_____

_____

_____

_____

_____

_____

_____

_____

_____

NOTE: Refer to the bullet points under each Competency in the ETS/SBEC study guide. Analyze each bullet point, and synthesize it down to a paraphrase that is meaningful to you, using no more than 5 words. List those phrases in order on the lines above. It may help to number the bullet points and the lines above. When complete,

Key Words:

Indonesian Gamelan
African Drumming
Indian Raga
Cuban Salsa
American Folk Songs
American Work Songs
Jazz
Blues
Ragtime
Gospel
Country
Bluegrass
Tejano

D E S C R I P T O R   H I G H L I G H T S

- Recognizes non-Western musical styles and understands their cultural derivation.
- Describes the characteristics of non-Western music according to genre, style, culture, or historical period.
- Understands the significance of composers and other contributors to the non-Western musical tradition.
- Analyzes and classifies examples of non-Western music by genre, style, culture, or historical period.

- Understands the important historical, social, artistic, and cultural events impacting the development of non-Western musical styles.
- Recognizes and describes music that reflects the heritage of the United States and Texas.
- Analyzes the purposes and roles of music in society and culture.
- Comprehends the relationship between music and society, culture, and technology.

7. Culture and Music

Competency 7:

The teacher understands music of diverse genres, styles, and cultures and knows how music can reflect elements of a specific society or culture.

A. NON-WESTERN MUSIC

- Indonesian gamelan - orchestra of metal and bamboo xylophones, gongs, and drums; orchestra performs alone or as accompaniment to dances, theatre, or puppet shows; music uses simple repeated melodies
- African drumming - drumming, singing, and dancing performed in a circular formation; drum ensemble instruments usually include various sizes and shapes of drums, as well as bells and rattles
- Indian raga - the rag is a seven note scale that forms the melodic basis for Indian music; the tal is the repeated rhythmic pattern, also very complex; the raga and tala are then used by the skilled Indian musician for creative improvisation; the most famous Indian musical instruments are the sitar and the tabla
- Cuban salsa - a dance influenced by the mambo, rhumba, jazz, bomba, turn patterns from the hustle, and one's own personal style; a unique New York phenomenon with the flavor of music from the Caribbean, Latin America, the Far East, and Europe; the New York Puerto Ricans have elevated the dance and the music to the highest level of performance and social art

B. UNITED STATES AND TEXAS MUSICAL HERITAGE

- American folk songs - musical works of a narrative nature that exist in oral tradition and were the sources for early popular music; examples include patriotic songs, soldiering songs, home songs
- American work songs - songs derived and developed from association with various occupations; examples include cowboy songs, sea shanties; railroad songs; prison work songs
- Jazz music - music involving lively, syncopated rhythms and instrumental improvisation; developed around the beginning of the 20th century; close connection to New Orleans as a cultural center before spreading to Northern cities
- Blues music - developed among rural, Southern blacks after the Civil War, giving expression to an exploited people; originally sung a cappella and later was accompanied by guitar; performed with a variety of groans, scoops, and bent notes; favored "blue" notes were the lowered 3rd, 5th, and 7th of the major scale
- Ragtime music - originated in the "cakewalk" (a couple's dance marked by strutting and acrobatic movements popular in the minstrel shows); featured syncopation against a regular bass rhythm; essentially music for piano solo, but the style was also used in early dance bands.
- Gospel music - traditional gospel music followed the "call and response" pattern of work songs sung by the slaves in the cotton fields; led to the practice of "lining out" songs where the leader sings first and the congregation responds; gospel music further developed into quartet singing, based on the close harmonies of the "barbershop quartet"; modern gospel uses a style of syncopated rhythm played on drums and translated to the key board or piano
- Country music - music based on hillbilly combined with Western cowboy themes; typically the singers strum the accompaniment on guitar; bands eventually formed that were dominated by violins and electric and steel guitars
- Bluegrass music - music developed in Kentucky; predominant instruments include violin, mandolin, guitar, and banjo; uses driving, syncopated rhythms along with close, high-pitched lead and harmony vocals

Continued

7. Culture and Music

· ·

- Tejano music - music of Texas Mexican youth based on the "conjunto" tradition (a polka feel with an accordian accompaniment, along with the bajo sexto 12 string bass guitar and violin); it is a blend of the "conjunto" tradition with pop, country, and rock and roll influences

D. MUSIC IN SOCIETY AND CULTURE
- Music as a tool for releasing emotions and expressing feelings
- Music as a tool for understanding and appreciating aesthetic expressions in the world
- Music as a tool for entertainment and personal enjoyment
- Music as a tool for communication within a society or culture
- Music as a tool for understanding symbology within a discipline or across disciplines
- Music as a tool for physical involvement expressed in a creative and artistic environment
- Music as a tool for teaching social and cultural mores and norms
- Music as a tool for teaching the continuity and stability of culture
- Music as a tool for teaching both independence and interdependence

E. MUSIC AND TECHNOLOGY
- Technology as a tool for teaching music reading skills
- Technology as a tool for teaching ear training skills
- Technology as a tool for teaching theoretical concepts in music
- Technology as a tool for teaching music history and culture
- Technology as a tool for composing and arranging music
- Technology as a tool for music rehearsal and performance practice
- Technology as a tool for research in music through the Internet

Domain IV:
Music Classroom Performance
Competencies 8-10
(25% of the test)

Music EC-12 Standard I:

The music teacher has a comprehensive visual and aural knowledge of musical perception and performance.

Music EC-12 Standard II:

The music teacher sings and plays a musical instrument.

Music EC-12 Standard V:

The music teacher has a comprehensive knowledge of music history and the relationship of music to history, society, and culture.

Music EC-12 Standard VI:

The music teacher applies a comprehensive knowledge of music to evaluate musical compositions, performances, and experiences.

Music EC-12 Standard VII:

The music teacher understands how to plan and implement effective music instruction and provides students with learning experiences that enhance their musical knowledge, skills, and appreciation.

Music EC-12 Standard IX:

The music teacher understands student assessment and uses assessment r esults to design instruction and promote student progress.

Music EC-12 Standard X:

The music teacher understands professional responsibilities and interactions relevant to music instruction and the school music program.

8. Vocal Performance

Key Descriptors:

_____

_____

_____

_____

_____

_____

_____

_____

_____

_____

_____

_____

_____

_____

_____

_____

NOTE: Refer to the bullet points under each Competency in the ETS/SBEC study guide. Analyze each bullet point, and synthesize it down to a paraphrase that is meaningful to you, using no more than 5 words. List those phrases in order on the lines above. It may help to number the bullet points and the lines above. When complete,

Key Words:

Foundations of Proper Singing

Vocal Mechanism

Vocal Classification, Ranges, Registers

Vocal Maturation

Vocal Diction

Vocal Health

Vocal Literature

Sight-Reading Methods

Choral Performance Criteria-
Phrasing, Intonation, Blend, Balance

Correcting Vocal Faults

D E S C R I P T O R   H I G H L I G H T S

- Understands the foundational principles of proper vocal technique.
- Understands the production of vocal sound.
- Knows proper vocal health techniques and stages of vocal maturation.
- Understands the basic concepts of vocal diction.
- Chooses appropriate vocal literature for the solo and small ensemble singer.
- Chooses appropriate choral literature for the larger ensemble.

- Chooses appropriate sight-reading methods.
- Understands the concepts of phrasing, intonation, blend and balance.
- Diagnoses performance problems and offers meaningful solutions for correcting vocal faults.
- Understand the use of constructive criticism in evaluating performance skills.

8. Vocal Performance

Competency 8:

The teacher demonstrates knowledge of methods and techniques for singing.

A thorough knowledge and understanding of proper pedagogy for voices and instruments, along with the use of correct conducting techniques, are necessary for a teacher to be successful in the music classroom in grades EC-12. The teacher must be skilled in diagnosing problems and prescribing appropriate and correct solutions to ensure quality instruction and learning. Implementing the appropriate technical foundation is fundamental for both individual students and the overall music program to achieve the desired positive results.

A. FOUNDATIONS OF PROPER SINGING
- Posture (Seated and Standing)
- Breathing
- Open Throat
- Vertical Vowel Alignment
- Articulation

B. VOCAL MECHANISM
- Activator-Breath; diaphragmatic breathing
- Vibrator-Vocal Cords; larynx and pharynx
- Resonators-Head (mouth, nose, sinuses), Throat, and Chest
- Articulators-Lips, Tongue, Teeth, Jaw, Hard and Soft Palates

C. VOCAL CLASSIFICATION, RANGES, AND REGISTERS
(Vocal registers are generally referred to as head voice and chest voice; other terminology includes "whistle register," falsetto, passaggio, and the "vocal fry".)

- Soprano-the highest female voice type; voice types include coloratura, lyric, dramatic; the range is roughly an octave below and above b prime
- Mezzo-Soprano-the middle female voice type; the range is roughly an octave below and above g prime
- Alto-the lowest female voice type; also called contralto; the range is roughly an octave below and above e prime
- Tenor-highest male voice type; voice types include lyric and helden-tenor; the range is roughly an octave below and above a
- Baritone-the middle male voice type; the range is roughly an octave below and above f
- Bass-the lowest male voice type; profundo, cantante, buffo; the range is roughly an octave below and above d

D. VOCAL MATURATION
- Child Voice-small range; flute-like, head tone voice quality
- Cambiata-puberty; care of the changing voice; attention to appropriate voice range; frequent monitoring of the voice
- Mature Voice-more extended range; greater stability of the vocal mechanism and vocal control; production still based on head tone voice quality

E. VOCAL DICTION
- English
- Latin
- Italian
- German
- French
- Spanish

F. VOCAL HEALTH
- Hydration
- Overuse/Abuse of Speaking and Singing Voice
- Illness
- Medications

8. Vocal Performance, cont'd.

G. SIGHT-READING METHODS
- Solfege Syllables/Hand Signs (Curwen)
- Scale-Step Numbers

H. VOCAL LITERATURE
- Solo Singer
- Small Ensemble
- Large Ensemble

I. CHORAL PERFORMANCE CRITERIA
- Phrasing
- Balance
- Blend
- Intonation

J. DIAGNOSING AND CORRECTING VOCAL FAULTS
- Posture and breathing
- Range extension and flexibility
- Register changes
- Breathy, strident, tense tone production
- Vibrato
- Intonation (proper vowel formation)
- Diction

**Domain IV:
Competencies 8-10**

9. Instrumental Performance

Key Descriptors:

_____

_____

_____

_____

_____

_____

_____

_____

_____

_____

_____

_____

_____

_____

_____

_____

NOTE: Refer to the bullet points under each Competency in the ETS/SBEC study guide. Analyze each bullet point, and synthesize it down to a paraphrase that is meaningful to you, using no more than 5 words. List those phrases in order on the lines above. It may help to number the bullet points and the lines above. When complete,

Key Words:

Foundations of Proper Playing Technique

Transpositions, Ranges, Registers

Instrument Maintenance

Instrumental Literature

Instrumental Performance Criteria - Phrasing, Intonation, Blend, Balance, Articulation

Correcting Instrument Technique Faults

DESCRIPTOR HIGHLIGHTS

- Understands foundational principles of proper playing technique for a range of instruments (general music, band, orchestra).
- Understands performance skills for a range of instruments (general music, band, orchestra).
- Knows transpositions, registers, and ranges for all instruments.
- Understands proper care and usage for a range of instruments (general music, band, orchestra).

- Chooses appropriate instrumental literature (solo, small ensemble, large ensemble).
- Understands the concepts of articulation, vibrato, intonation, blend, balance, and phrasing for the instrumentalist.
- Diagnoses performance problems and offers meaningful solutions for correcting technical faults.

9. Instrumental Performance

Competency 9:

The teacher demonstrates knowledge of methods and techniques for playing musical instruments.

A. FOUNDATIONS OF INSTRUMENTAL TECHNIQUE

- Woodwinds (flute, piccolo, clarinet, bass clarinet, oboe, English horn, bassoon, saxophone)
  Posture; breathing; position of head and hands; embouchure; mouthpieces and reeds, tonguing; fingering; tuning and instrument tendencies
- Brass (trumpet, trombone, French horn, euphonium, tuba)
  Posture; breathing; position of head and hands; embouchure; mouthpieces; mutes; attack; tubing; tonguing; fingering and positioning; tuning and instrument tendencies
- Percussion (non-pitched and pitched)
  Mallets and sticks; hand position (grip); use of wrist; playing area of instrument; timpani tuning
- Strings (violin, viola, cell, string bass, harp) Instrument design; bow construction; posture; position of right and left hands; bowing techniques; harmonics
- Keyboard Instruments
  Types and uses of keyboard instruments for the classroom; maintenance; playing techniques; keyboard labs and their uses
- Instruments for General Music (recorders, autoharp, guitar, Orff instruments, classroom rhythm instruments)

B. TRANSPOSITIONS, RANGES, AND REGISTERS

(In instrumental music, these vary depending on the individual instrument; all are affected by the normal clef for each instrument; transpositions depend on whether that instrument plays in the concert key or is a transposing instrument.)

C. INSTRUMENTAL MAINTENANCE - CARE AND USAGE OF INSTRUMENTS

- Assembly
- Cleaning
- Storage
- Pads, Corks, Oils, and other Lubricants
- Reeds
- Rosin
- Bow Maintenance
- General Repairs

D. INSTRUMENTAL LITERATURE

- Solo
- Small ensemble
- Large ensemble

E. INSTRUMENTAL PERFORMANCE CRITERIA

(Pertains to stylistic performance practices appropriate to historical periods of music and also to various instrumental and vocal ensembles, as well as solo performance.)

- Phrasing
- Blend
- Balance
- Intonation
- Articulation

F. DIAGNOSIS AND CORRECTION OF INSTRUMENTAL FAULTS

- Posture and breathing
- Embouchure
- Fingerings
- Bowing techniques; shifting (orchestral instruments)
- Characteristic tone production
- Range extension and flexibility
- Register changes
- Articulation
- Vibrato (depending on instrument)
- Intonation

10. Conducting

Key Descriptors:

_____

_____

_____

_____

_____

_____

_____

_____

_____

_____

_____

_____

_____

_____

_____

_____

NOTE: Refer to the bullet points under each Competency in the ETS/SBEC study guide. Analyze each bullet point, and synthesize it down to a paraphrase that is meaningful to you, using no more than 5 words. List those phrases in order on the lines above. It may help to number the bullet points and the lines above. When complete,

Key Words:

Conducting Patterns
Cuing Techniques
Expressive Techniques
Small Ensemble Techniques
Large Ensemble Techniques
Musical Interpretation
Performance Styles
Vocal Music Repertoire
Instrumental Music Repertoire
Legal/Ethical Performance Issues
Copyright Laws
Music Education Policies/Guidelines

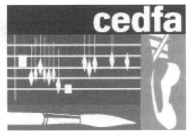

The American Society of Composers, Authors and Publishers

D E S C R I P T O R   H I G H L I G H T S

- Uses appropriate conducting techniques for small and large ensembles.
- Understands basic conducting patterns, cuing techniques, and expressive techniques.
- Chooses correct vocal and instrumental performance techniques for small and large ensembles.
- Understands musical interpretation and demonstrates knowledge of musical styles and performance practices.

- Chooses appropriate and varied repertoire for vocal and instrumental ensembles.
- Understands legal and ethical issues related to the use of music in an educational setting.
- Understands copyright laws as they apply to the educational environment.
- Understands federal, state, and local policies governing musical performances in an educational setting.

10. Conducting

Competency 10:

The teacher knows how to conduct vocal and instrumental performances.

A. CONDUCTING PATTERNS

- 2/4
- 3/4
- 4/4
- 6/8
- 9/8
- 12/8
- Asymmetrical meters
- Terminology - ictus, tactus, anacrusis

B. CUING TECHNIQUES

- Usually the left hand cues entrances of instruments or voices and indicates expressive qualities
- The right hand indicates the beat

C. EXPRESSIVE TECHNIQUES

- Use of the body in cuing
- Facial expression of the conductor
- Relative size of gestures

D. MUSICAL INTERPRETATION AND PERFORMANCE STYLES

- Score markings and indications (especially if from the composer and not editorial)
- Historical background (composer and stylistic period)
- Musical elements
- Relationship of parts
- Conducting considerations
- Text in vocal music

E. REPERTOIRE (VOCAL AND INSTRUMENTAL)

- Age and ability level of the performers
- Size of group
- Voicing of ensemble (number of performers on a part)
- Level of difficulty in all sections of the music
- Level of difficulty in the accompaniment
- Text considerations in vocal music
- Variety of styles and genres represented
- Potential audiences and performance venues

F. LEGAL AND ETHICAL ISSUES

- State ethics code for all teachers
- Code of Ethics and Standard Practices (TMEA)
- Responsibilities to the profession

- Responsibilities to the student
- Responsibilities to the community

G. COPYRIGHT LAW

- Copyright Act of 1976
- "Fair Use" clause for educators
- Permission from publisher to arrange music
- Permission/fee for recording music
- Application to the music classroom
- Application to music technology
- Royalties for musicals and other shows

H. MUSIC EDUCATION POLICIES/ GUIDELINES

- Federal
  - No Child Left Behind (NCLB) Act of 2001 (PL 107-110)
  - Individuals With Disabilities Education Act of 1975 (PL 94-142)
  - Copyright Act of 1976
  - Music Educators National Conference (MENC)
  - Advocacy and Coalition Efforts

- State
  - State Legislative Policies
  - Texas Education Agency (TEA)
  - Texas Music Educators Association (TMEA)
  - University Interscholastic League (UIL)
  - Center for Educator Development in the Fine Arts (CEDFA)
  - Advocacy and Coalition Efforts

- Local
  - School Board Policies
  - Advocacy and Coalition Efforts

Domain V:
Music Education
Competencies 11-12
(17% of the test)

Music EC-12 Standard V:

The music teacher has a comprehensive knowledge of music history and the relationship of music to history, society, and culture.

Music EC-12 Standard VII:

The music teacher understands how to plan and implement effective music instruction and provides students with learning experiences that enhance their musical knowledge, skills, and appreciation.

Music EC-12 Standard VIII:

The music teacher understands and applies appropriate management and discipline strategies for the music class.

Music EC-12 Standard IX:

The music teacher understands student assessment and uses assessment results to design instruction and promote student progress.

11. Instruction

Key Descriptors:

_____

_____

_____

_____

_____

_____

_____

_____

_____

_____

_____

_____

_____

_____

_____

NOTE: Refer to the bullet points under each Competency in the ETS/SBEC study guide. Analyze each bullet point, and synthesize it down to a paraphrase that is meaningful to you, using no more than 5 words. List those phrases in order on the lines above. It may help to number the bullet points and the lines above. When complete,

Key Words:

Texas Essential Knowledge and Skills (TEKS)

Assessment

Sequencing

Special Needs, Learning Modalities, Levels of Development

Fundamental Principles of Music

Music Making (Instruments and Voice)

Musical Styles and Genres

Music Evaluation

Materials and Resources

Technology in the Music Classroom

Critical Thinking and Problem-Solving Skills

TEKS

DESCRIPTOR HIGHLIGHTS

- Demonstrates knowledge of content and performance standards as outlined in the Texas Essential Knowledge and Skills TEKS).
- Recognizes the significance of the TEKS in developing a music curriculum.
- Uses multiple forms of assessment in order to determine student progress and develop instructional plans.
- Understands the importance of sequencing and delivery of music instruction that encourages active participation in learning and makes content meaningful.
- Adapts instructional methods for students with varied needs, learning modalities, levels of development, and musical experience.

- Provides students with varied activities in making music using instruments and voices.
- Allows students to respond to a wide range of musical styles and genres and evaluate compositions and performances.
- Understands the importance of appropriate materials and resources available for the music classroom.
- Understands the use of technology as a teaching and learning tool in the music classroom.
- Provides students with frequent opportunities to use critical thinking and problem solving skills in analyzing, creating, and responding to music.

11. Instruction

Competency 11:

The teacher knows how to plan and implement effective music instruction.

Planning and implementing effective music instruction and age appropriate activities in the music classroom is the primary basis for success as a music teacher. A thorough and comprehensive knowledge base and the ability to translate that knowledge into meaningful instruction tied to student achievement is the hallmark of great teaching. Coupled with outstanding teaching ability is the need for expert organizational and management skill in setting up an efficient and effective classroom environment.

A. TEXAS ESSENTIAL KNOWLEDGE AND SKILLS (TEKS)
- Perception
- Creative Expression/Performance
- Historical/Cultural Heritage
- Response/Evaluation
- Senate Bill 815-requires that the TEKS be used as a basis for music instruction offered in the public schools in Texas

B. ASSESSMENT
- Performance Based Demonstrations
- Cooperative Learning Groups
- Written and Oral Tests
- Discussion/Observation
- Rubrics
- Interviews
- Self-Assessment
- Peer Assessment
- Teacher Self-Assessment
- Benchmark Testing
- Portfolios
- Reporting to Parents

C. SEQUENCING
- Planning begins with age, ability level, modalities, learning styles, special needs
- Presentation of concepts moves from simple to more complex (spiral curriculum)
- Effective teaching strategies must include a well-paced lesson, varied activities, positive feedback, aural reinforcement, opportunities for repetition and rehearsal, and opening and closing activities that motivate the learner
- Taxonomy of Educational Objectives (Cognitive and Affective - Benjamin Bloom; Psychomotor - Elizabeth Simpson)
- Structure of Knowledge-Lynn Erickson

D. SPECIAL NEEDS, LEARNING MODALITIES, LEVELS OF DEVELOPMENT
- Mainstreaming, Inclusion, Least Restrictive Environment (PL 94-142, 1976)
- Modifications (Individualized Education Plan-IEP)
- Admission, Review, Dismissal (ARD)
- Modalities-Aural, Visual, Tactile-Kinesthetic
- Learning Styles (Dunn and Dunn Model)
- Multiple Intelligences (Gardner)
- Brain Based Learning (Jenson)
- Developmental Stages (Piaget and Bruner)

E. FUNDAMENTAL PRINCIPLES OF MUSIC
- Rhythm
- Texture (Harmony)
- Dynamics
- Melody
- Timbre
- Form

F. MUSIC MAKING FOR INSTRUMENTS AND VOICES
- Singing
- Moving
- Playing Instruments
- Listening
- Creating
- Reading

11. Instruction (Planning and Implementing), cont'd.

G. MUSICAL STYLES AND GENRES (SEE DOMAIN III: MUSIC HISTORY AND CULTURE)
- Assists students in understanding the role of music in history
- Connects music to other arts and disciplines, technology, and aspects of cultural life

H. MUSIC EVALUATION - Assist students in developing criteria for making value judgments and informed choices concerning music performance

I. MATERIALS AND RESOURCES (CURRICULUM)
- National Music Standards (MENC)
- Texas Essential Knowledge and Skills (TEKS)
- Kodaly
- Orff
- Dalcroze (Eurhythmics)
- Gordon (Music Learning Theory)
- Suzuki (Talent Education)
- Comprehensive Musicianship
- Manhattanville Music Curriculum Project (Spiral Curriculum)
- Curriculum Guides, Music Series Textbooks, Technology

12. Learning Experiences in Music

Key Descriptors:

_____

_____

_____

_____

_____

_____

_____

_____

_____

_____

_____

_____

_____

_____

NOTE: Refer to the bullet points under each Competency in the ETS/SBEC study guide. Analyze each bullet point, and synthesize it down to a paraphrase that is meaningful to you, using no more than 5 words. List those phrases in order on the lines above. It may help to number the bullet points and the lines above. When complete,

Key Words:

Relevance of Music Skills/
   Lifelong Enjoyment of Music

Personal Experiences with Music

Independent Music Study

Music-related Career Options
Music as a Vocation/Avocation

World Music Appreciation

Fine Arts Integration

Organization and Management of
   Classroom Music

Music Classroom Inventory

Concert Etiquette

D E S C R I P T O R   H I G H L I G H T S

- Assists students in developing musical skills that are relevant and meaningful to their lives.
- Provides students with a level of musical skill that encourages lifelong involvement in music.
- Provides students with opportunities to draw on personal musical experiences.
- Encourages students to pursue musical knowledge and skills independently.
- Recognizes the importance of music-related career options and assists students in exploring these possibilities.
- Understands the importance of music as a vocation/avocation.
- Assists students in understanding and appreciating all

cultures by incorporating a diverse music repertoire, includ ing music from both Western and Non-Western traditions.
- Understands the importance of integrating music with other fine arts and subjects.
- Effectively organizes and administrates the music classroom in various settings by managing time, instructional resources, and physical space.
- Applies strategies for managing and documenting music classroom inventory (library, textbooks, uniforms, instruments, other equipment).
- Assists students in understanding and demonstrating acceptable concert etiquette.

12. Learning Experiences in Music

Competency 12:

The teacher knows how to provide students with learning experiences that enhance their musical knowledge, skills, and appreciation.

A. RELEVANCE OF MUSIC SKILLS/ LIFELONG ENJOYMENT OF MUSIC

- Music as emotional expression, for aesthetic enjoyment, as entertainment, as communication, for physical response, as symbolic representation. Music used to validate civic and religious rituals, to express culture, to integrate society (bring people together)

B. PERSONAL EXPERIENCES WITH MUSIC

- This includes all experiences in music and the arts outside the school setting
- Students may draw on these experiences to enrich the teaching and learning environment in the public school classroom

C. INDEPENDENT MUSIC STUDY

- Private lessons
- Auditioning for civic/community productions
- Research (Internet and Library)
- Participation in outside music groups

D. MUSIC-RELATED CAREER OPTIONS (VOCATION AND AVOCATION)

- Teaching/Administration
- Performance
- Church Music
- Music Business
- Composing/Arranging
- Writing/Publishing
- Conducting

E. WORLD MUSIC APPRECIATION

- Multiethnic Music Education - curriculum development that focuses exclusively on the study of groups distinguished by ethnic origin
- World Music Education - the study of musical elements as they are treated in various music styles around the world
- Repertoire Selection - introduces students to the diverse music traditions of Western and Non-Western music

F. FINE ARTS INTEGRATION - an approach that respects the integrity of each discipline while showing the connections and commonalities among them

- Music and the other fine arts (visual arts, theatre, dance)
- Music and other disciplines (language arts, math, science, social studies, physical education, foreign language)
- Integration Models (thematic web, threaded, immersed)

G. ORGANIZATION AND MANAGEMENT OF THE MUSIC CLASSROOM

- Managing time, space, instructional resources
- Managing student behaviors
- Managing paperwork and record keeping

H. MUSIC CLASSROOM INVENTORY

- Music Library
- Textbooks
- Uniforms
- Instruments
- Technology Equipment
- Other Music Equipment

I. CONCERT ETIQUETTE

- Perceptive listening
- Developing positive attitudes toward music
- Understanding appropriate behaviors in classical concert settings
- Showing proper respect for conductors and performers (applause, entering and exiting during a performance, remaining silent)

Appendix I

Tips and Study Aids

53

Tips for Passing the TExES Exam

1. There are two testing periods in a day; you need to request one test per testing period if possible.

2. Get to the exam an hour or two early; the directions they send out are usually a little confusing, and you don't want to be rushed or upset.

3. Take two forms of ID, one has to have your picture on it.

4. Take three or more number 2 pencils.

5. Bring a receipt or any other form of confirmation of registration you might have.

6. During the practice tests and the real tests mark the important details in both the questions and the answers. Always mark any questions you are not sure of.

7. Divide the number of questions by the number of hours allowed to determine how much time you have for each question.

8. Write down your acronym (see Appendix 1) and brief Competency information on your test booklet prior to the test. When answering each question, if you get stuck, refer to the acronym which may help you recall content from the Competency the question is from, which will help you determine the answer.

9. Read all of the answers before making your selection.

10. Answers to questions: Two are remotely correct and two are reasonably correct. Use your critical thinking skills and pick the best answer.

11. After you complete the test there is usually plenty of time to double-check your answers. Always put a mark of some type beside any answers you are not sure of, so that afterward you can double-check your responses.

IMPORTANT NOTE: Follow the Steps for Success on page 10 and 11 of this manual.

Appendix I
Tips and Study Aids

Acronym

This study program involves the use of an acronym for easy memorization. If the acronym below is not to your liking, simply change it to an acronym that works for you.

NOTE:

> DOMAIN I has 3 Competencies: 1-3 (approximately 25% of the test)
> DOMAIN II has 2 Competencies: 4-5 (approximately 17% of the test)
> DOMAIN III has 2 Competencies: 6-7 (approximately 17% of the test)
> DOMAIN IV has 3 Competencies: 8-10 (approximately 25% of the test)
> DOMAIN V has 2 Competencies: 11-12 (approximately 17% of the test)

As you use the worksheets keep the acronym in mind-it will help you remember the Key Titles. The numbers and letters by the Domains below refer to the Key Titles seen on the next page and heading each Competency page. The letter is the first letter of the first word of the Key Title. The titles are descriptive of the Competency, and once you recall the Title, the Competency information should come back to you.

DOMAIN I: LISTENING	1. E **East** 2. S **South** 3. E **East (of)**
DOMAIN II: MUSIC THEORY AND COMPOSITION	4. N **North** 5. C **Carolina**
DOMAIN III: MUSIC HISTORY AND CULTURE	6. W **We** 7. C **Cross**
DOMAIN IV: MUSIC CLASSROOM PERFORMANCE	8. V **Virginia** 9. I **Indiana** 10. C **Connects (to)**
DOMAIN V: MUSIC EDUCATION	11. I **Illinois (through)** 12. LE **Logansport (and) Evansville**

SO...

East South East (of) North Carolina; We Cross Virginia; Indiana Connects (to) Illinois (through) Logansport (and) Evansville.

NOTE: This acronym-based phrase represents all 12 Competencies.

Competency Definitions

Domain I

1. **Elements**

   Competency 1:
   The teacher applies standard terminology to describe and analyze various elements in a musical recording.

2. **Styles and Genres**

   Competency 2:
   The teacher recognizes and describes music of diverse genres, styles, and cultures in a musical recording.

3. **Evaluation**

   Competency 3:
   The teacher evaluates and critiques musical compositions and performances in a musical recording.

Domain II

4. **Notation**

   Competency 4:
   The teacher knows how to read, write, and interpret standard music notation.

5. **Composition**

   Competency 5:
   The teacher understands methods and techniques of musical composition and improvisation and knows how to arrange music for specific purposes and settings.

Domain III

6. **Western Music**

   Competency 6:
   The teacher demonstrates a comprehensive knowledge of the history of Western music.

7. **Culture and Music**

   Competency 7:
   The teacher understands music of diverse genres, styles, and cultures and knows how music can reflect elements of a specific society or culture.

Domain IV

8. **Vocal Performance**

   Competency 8:
   The teacher demonstrates knowledge of methods and techniques for singing.

9. **Instrumental Performance**

   Competency 9:
   The teacher demonstrates knowledge of methods and techniques for playing musicalinstruments.

10. **Conducting**

    Competency 10:
    The teacher knows how to conduct vocal and instrumental performances.

Domain V

11. **Instruction (Planning and Implementing)**

    Competency 11:
    The teacher knows how to plan and implement effective music instruction.

12. **Learning Experiences in Music**

    Competency 12:
    The teacher knows how to provide students with learning experiences that enhance their musical knowledge, skills, and appreciation.

Appendix I
Tips and Study Aids

Practice Test Method

A very important part of your test preparation consists of learning how to assess your new found knowledge base. The best way to accomplish this is by using practice questions available for the TExES in the ETS/SBEC study manual and other sources. We recommend using our Practice Test Worksheet in Appendix III. You will want to copy this worksheet several times if you are working on question sets from other sources as well. The practice test in Appendix III is a sampling of the SBEC questions, and they are included in this book to illustrate how our practice test method works. The worksheet will teach you how to properly analyze questions. The process of this worksheet is explained below.

1   **Read each question, and if you wish, restate the question in your own words.** In other words... figure out what they are really asking you. Always read the question and all the choices of answers before restating the question in your own words.

2   **Determine what Competency** the question is referring to. If you look at the answer key to the sample questions in the SBEC manual, you will notice that the Competency number appears beside each answer. Each question refers to a particular Competency in the sample test and on the real test. Knowledge of the Competency information will help you answer questions. However, you must also consider the point of view of the SBEC to help you determine the answers.

3   **State why you think this is the correct Competency.** It is best to understand why you are making your choices. Expressing this in writing is part of your analysis process.

4   **State your answer. State why this is correct answer and why it connect to the Competency you chose.** It is important to understand why you are making the choices you are making.

5   **Look up the Competency and the answer in the answer key after completing each question.** If you missed the answer cross yours out and write the letter of the correct answer beside yours. If you missed the Competency number cross yours out and write the correct one beside that.

6   **Write down why you were wrong about the Competency, or answer, or both,** and why the answer key is correct. This is an important analysis which leads you to an understanding of the point of view of the SBEC. You may not agree with their point of view but choosing the answers that the SBEC would choose is important to your success on the test.

Continue through every question this way and by the end of the practice test you should be getting better at identifying the Competencies and choosing the correct answers.

Worksheet 1
Building the Acronym

List the first letter of each Key Title for each Competency. Study them on the Competency study pages in this manual, and then write them from memory here. The headings below are the Domain titles.

I. Listening

    1. _____

    2. _____

    3. _____

II. Music Theory and Composition

    4. _____

    5. _____

III. Music History and Culture

    6. _____

    7. _____

IV. Music Classroom Performance

    8. _____

    9. _____

    10. _____

V. Music Education

    11. _____

    12. _____

Worksheet 2
Competency Key Titles

List the Key Title for each Competency. Study them on the Competency study pages in this manual, and then write them from memory here.

I.   Listening
    1. _____
    2. _____
    3. _____

II. Music Theory and Composition
    4. _____
    5. _____

III. Music History and Culture
    6. _____
    7. _____

IV. Music Classroom Performance
    8. _____
    9. _____
    10. _____

V.   Music Education
    11. _____
    12. _____

Appendix I
Tips and Study Aids

Worksheet 3
Competency Definitions

State each Competency definition in your own words. Use conversational language, like "When I am teaching, I..." You might even want to memorize these definitions in your wording instead of the SBEC definitions. You can use simpler wording, use additional words, etc. NOTE: Personalizing these definitions will help you understand them.

1. _____

2. _____

3. _____

4. _____

5. _____

6. _____

7. _____

8. _____

9. _____

10. _____

11. _____

12. _____

Worksheet 4
Key Descriptors

See the Descriptor exercise starting on p. 14 and in each Competency section. Write down your Key Descriptor phrases for each Descriptive Statement under all Competency headings below. (Refer to the TExES ETS/SBEC manual for the bullet points under each Competency to create your Descriptor phrases.) On each Competency section below there is space for you to write your Key Descriptor phrases. Copy when complete and carry with you for additional study.

Competency 1

_____
_____
_____
_____
_____
_____
_____
_____
_____
_____
_____
_____
_____
_____
_____
_____

Competency 3

_____
_____
_____
_____
_____
_____
_____
_____
_____
_____
_____
_____
_____
_____
_____
_____

Competency 5

_____
_____
_____
_____
_____
_____
_____
_____
_____
_____
_____
_____
_____
_____
_____
_____

Competency 2

_____
_____
_____
_____
_____
_____
_____
_____
_____
_____
_____
_____
_____
_____
_____
_____

Competency 4

_____
_____
_____
_____
_____
_____
_____
_____
_____
_____
_____
_____
_____
_____
_____
_____

Competency 6

_____
_____
_____
_____
_____
_____
_____
_____
_____
_____
_____
_____
_____
_____
_____
_____

Worksheet 4
Key Descriptors, cont'd.

Competency 7

_____
_____
_____
_____
_____
_____
_____
_____
_____
_____
_____
_____
_____
_____

Competency 9

_____
_____
_____
_____
_____
_____
_____
_____
_____
_____
_____
_____
_____
_____

Competency 11

_____
_____
_____
_____
_____
_____
_____
_____
_____
_____
_____
_____
_____
_____

Competency 8

_____
_____
_____
_____
_____
_____
_____
_____
_____
_____
_____
_____
_____
_____

Competency 10

_____
_____
_____
_____
_____
_____
_____
_____
_____
_____
_____
_____
_____
_____

Competency 12

_____
_____
_____
_____
_____
_____
_____
_____
_____
_____
_____
_____
_____
_____

Appendix I
Tips and Study Aids

Worksheet 5
Study Assignments

1. RECALL THE INFORMATION:

   "Know what you know, and know what you don't know."

   Once during your study, take blank pieces of paper and write down everything you know about the Competencies (at least the ones you feel weakest in). You might include:

   a) Competency definitions

   b) Key Words for each Competency

   c) Important concepts you can recall about each Competency

2. REWRITE THE QUESTIONS:

   This is a one-time assignment: Re-write 5 questions in your own words. Do not read the scenario or answers. Simply restate the questions. Most people misinterpret certain types of questions. This exercise helps identify which types of questions may throw you off. If you are unsure about what a question is actually asking you on the test, it can be very helpful if you rewrite it.

3. PRACTICE TESTS:

   There are practice test questions in the Study Manual from ETS/SBEC and a sampling of them in the back of this manual. See the "Practice Test Method" in Appendix I of this manual for complete instructions on answering practice questions. Make several copies of the "Practice Test Worksheet" in Appendix III and use it for a practice test answer sheet or use blank sheets of paper. There are other sources for questions—through your university, ACP, or from other publishers' TExES books. The most important step on the worksheet in Appendix III is the last step...it asks you why the test writers chose the answer that they did. This is a critical step in the process of aligning your thoughts and behavior with the SBEC point of view...what the test is based on.

4. ANALYZE STRENGTHS AND WEAKNESSES:

   Review which Competencies you are the weakest in from your sample results. Do extra study on those areas. (Remember, correct reasons for choosing answers is KEY...simply picking the answer for wrong reasons will not help you on the REAL test.)

GOOD LUCK!

Appendix II

Resources and References

Recommended Classical Listening List
Domain I: Listening

These listening selections are strongly recommended for those preparing for the TExES exam. While examinees should be thoroughly familiar with these particular pieces, composers, and representative styles, this is not an inclusive list of listening material that may be encountered on the actual TExES test.

Middle Ages/Renaissance

Anonymous	Selected Gregorian Chants
Machaut	Agnus Dei Mass
Josquin des Prez	Pange Lingua Mass
Palestrina	Pope Marcellus Mass
Palestrina	Selected motets
Vittoria	Selected motets
Gesualdo, Monteverdi	Selected madrigals (early)

> **TIP:**
> An easy way to listen to selections: Go to www.amazon.com and enter the selection title in the search window. Often there are samples of selections available for listening on this site.

Baroque

Monteverdi	Orfeo; L'Incoronazione di Poppea
Gabrieli, G.	Symphonie sacrae; Sonata pian e forte; In ecclesiis (motet)
Purcell	Dido and Aeneas
Vivaldi	Gloria; The Seasons
Handel	Messiah
Bach	Brandenburg Concertos; Keyboard pieces; Cantatas; Passions; Mass in B Minor

Classical

Haydn	String Quartets; Symphonies
Mozart	Symphonies; Operas; Requiem
Beethoven	Symphonies; Piano Sonatas; String Quartets

Romantic

Schubert	Art Songs; Symphonies; Piano pieces
Schumann	Art Songs; Symphonies; Piano pieces
Berlioz	Symphonie Fantastique
Chopin	Piano Pieces
Mendelssohn	Symphonies; Overtures; Piano Pieces

Continued

Appendix II
Resources and References

Recommended Classical Listening List
Domain I: Listening

Romantic, continued

Liszt	Piano pieces; Les Preludes
Verdi	Operas; Requiem
Wagner	Tristan und Isolde (prelude); Other Music Dramas
Brahms	Symphonies; Piano Pieces; Requiem
Tchaikovsky	Ballets; Piano concertos
Strauss	Art Songs; Tone Poems
Mahler	Symphonies; Das Lied von der Erde
Mussorgsky	Pictures at an Exhibition (piano and orchestral)
Saint-Saens	Carnival of the Animals; Danse Macabre

Modern

Debussy	La Mer; Prelude a l'apres-midi d'un faune; Piano pieces
Puccini	Operas
Ives	Variations on America; Concord Sonata
Schoenberg	Pierrot Lunaire
Berg	Wozzeck
Webern	Symphony, Op. 21
Stravinsky	Ballets; Symphony of Psalms
Prokofiev	Peter and the Wolf
Gershwin	Rhapsody in Blue; American in Paris; Porgy and Bess; Piano pieces
Copland	Appalachian Spring; Ballets
Varese	Ionisation
Bartok	Music for Strings, Percussion, and Celesta
Orff	Carmina Burana
Britten	War Requiem; Ceremony of Carols; Operas
Cage	Music of Changes; Prepared piano pieces
Messiaen	Quartet for the End of Time
Bernstein	West Side Story; Chichester Psalms
Crumb	Ancient Voices of Children
Glass	Einstein on the Beach
Babbitt	Concerto for Piano and Orchestra
Adams	Phrygian Gates; Nixon in China

Non-Western/American Music Styles
Domain I: Listening

Listening examples from the following styles are strongly recommended in preparing for the listening portion of the TExES exam. This is not an inclusive list of listening material that may be encountered on the actual TExES test.

See the References by Domain section in this manual for suggested CD sets.

Non-Western Music   **American Music**

Indonesian gamelan   Native American   Gospel
African drumming   American folk-songs   Country Western
Indian raga   American work songs   Bluegrass
Cuban salsa   Spirituals   Tejano
Oriental/Asian influence Jazz   Mariachi
Celtic influence   Blues
Caribbean/Calypso influence   Ragtime

Aural Skills – Domain I: Listening

The following list represents types of aural skills that participants may be asked to identify on the listening portion of the music TExES exam. This is not an inclusive list of all aural skills that may be encountered on the actual TExES exam.

For practicing these skills, participants should find a partner to play examples from the list below or review these skills using technology software programs suggested in the Reference by Domain section of this manual.

Aural Skills Categories

Rhythmic Patterns (syncopation, hemiola, augmentation, diminution, contour, sequence, repetition)
Intervals (ascending and descending)
Scales (including pentatonic, whole-tone, modes, blues)
Cadences (PAC, IAC, Plagal, Half, Deceptive)
Chordal Structures (Major, Minor, Augmented, Diminished, Dominant 7th, Diminished 7th)
Textures (ostinato, doublings, melody and countermelody, monophonic, homophonic, Polyphonic)
Symbols and Terms (dynamic, embellishments, tempo markings, articulation markings)
Rhythmic and Melodic Error Detection (unison, two-three-and four parts or more in choral, band, and orchestral scores)

Terminology Checklist
Domain II: Music Theory and Composition

Pitch

Pitch
Key signature
Interval
Enharmonic
Relative keys
Parallel keys
Tonic
Supertonic
Mediant
Subdominant
Leading tone
Major scale
Natural minor scale
Harmonic minor scale
Melodic minor scale
Chromatic scale
Whole-tone scale
Pentatonic scale
Blues scale
Ionian mode
Dorian mode
Phrygian mode
Lydian mode
Mixolydian mode
Aeolian mode
Locrian mode
Overtone series
Harmonic series
Expressive marks
Pianissimo
Piano
Mezzo piano
Mezzo forte
Forte
Fortissimo
Crescendo
Decrescendo
Sforzando
Accent
Marcato
Staccato
Legato
Diminuendo

Rhythm

Rhythm
Beat
Tempo
Simple beat
Compound beat
Time signature
Meter
Duple meter
Triple meter
Quadruple meter
Syncopation
Tie
Slur
Homorhythm
Cross-rhythm
Polyrhythm
Largo
Lento
Adagio
Andante
Moderato
Allegretto
Allegro
Presto
Prestissimo
Ritard
Ritardando
Accelerando
Rubato
Augmentation
Diminution
Fermata
Tenuto

Tonality

Tonic
Consonance
Dissonance
Dyad
Triad
Root
Major
Minor
Augmented
Diminished
7th chord
9th/13th chords
Root position
Inversions
Figured bass
Tertian harmony
Quartal harmony
Quintal harmony
Chromaticism
Modulation
Pedal 6/4
Cadential 6/4
Passing 6/4
Secondary harmony
Secondary dominant
Altered chords
Borrowed chords
Italian Aug. 6th chord
French Aug. 6th chord
German Aug. 6th chord
Neopolitan chord
Tritone
Picardy third
Tonal
Atonal
Bitonal
Polytonal

Melody/Harmony/Form

Conjunct
Disjunct
Step
Skip
Diatonic
Non-diatonic
Motive
Leitmotif
Idee fixe
Phrase
Period
Antecedent
Consequent
Incipient
Cadence
Plagal cadence
Authentic cadence
Perfect authentic cadence
Imperfect authentic cadence
Half cadence
Deceptive cadence
Binary
Ternary
Rondo
Theme and variations
Ground bass
Passacaglia
Sonata-Allegro form
Exposition
Development
Recapitulation
Coda
Cadenza
Ritornello
Tutti
Ripieno
Concertino
Ornamentation
Embellishment
Tone row
Original row
Inverted row
Retrograde row
Retrograde inversion row
Serialism
12-tone technique
Dodecaphony
Caesura
D.C. al Fine
D.C. al Coda

Voice-Leading

Similar motion
Contrary motion
Parallel motion
Oblique motion
Open structure
Closed structure
Monody
Homophony
Polyphony
Fugue
Imitation
Inversion
Retrograde
Retrograde Inversion
Non-chord tones
Passing tone
Neighbor tone
Escape tone
Appoggiatura
Suspension
Anticipation
Pedal point

Know both definitions of terms and corresponding symbols.

Genres and Styles
Domain III: Music History and Culture

Middle Ages/Renaissance
Modality
Troubadours/Trouveres
Plainchant
Organum
Ars Antiqua
Ars Nova
Mass (Ordinary)
Motet
Chanson
Madrigal
Roman School
Venetian School
Florentine Camerata
    (into Baroque)

Baroque
Major/Minor Tonality
Terraced Dynamics
Concertato Principle
Da Capo Aria
Ornamentation
Opera
Ricercar
Canzona
Fugue

Classical
Absolute Music
Major/Minor Tonality
Symphonic Development
Growth of Orchestra
Role of Conductor
Sonata Allegro Form
Earliest Song Cycle
    (Beethoven)
Oratorio Developed
String Quartet

Romantic
Programmatic Music
Tone Poem/Symphonic Poem
Art Song/Song Cycle
Opera
Character Pieces (Piano)
String Quartet
Virtuoso Performers
Breakdown of
    Tonality/Chromaticism

Modern
Impressionism
Expressionism
Pointillism
Nationalism
Neo-Classicism
12-Tone Technique/
    Serialism/Dodecaphony
Primitivism
Aleatory/Chance
    Music/Indeterminacy
Minimalism
Electronic Music
Musique Concrete

Non-Western Music
Indonesian gamelan
African drumming
Indian raga
Cuban salsa
Oriental/Asian influence
Celtic influence
Caribbean/Calypso influence

American Music
Native American songs
Folk songs
Work songs
Spirituals
Jazz
Blues
Ragtime
Gospel
Country Western
Bluegrass
Tejano
Mariachi
Barbershop Quartet
Musical Theater

Pedagogy Topics
Domain IV: Music Classroom Performance

Vocal

- Posture
- Breath Support
- Open throat
- Vertical vowel alignment
- Clear Enunciation/Articulation
- Vibrator
- Activator
- Resonators
- Articulators
- Diction (Latin, English, Italian, German, French, Spanish)
- Ranges of voices
- Classification of voices
- Changing voice (cambiata)

Instrumental
Band

- Woodwinds
  Piccolo, Flute, Clarinet, Bass Clarinet, Oboe, English horn, Bassoon, Saxophone
- Brass
  Cornet, Trumpet, French horn, Trombone, Euphonium, Tuba
- Percussion
  Snare Drum, Timpani, Keyboard Mallet Instruments, Cymbals, Triangle, Tambourine, Chimes, Latin Percussion Instruments (bongos, claves, maracas, guiro, cowbell, cabasa, timbales, shakers, vibra-slap)
- Embouchure
- Tonguing
- Fingering
- Posture
- Breath Support
- Transposition (some instruments are transposing)
- Tuning
- Overtone Series
- Characteristic Sounds
- Mouthpieces

- Single and Double Reeds
- Valves
- Slides
- Bores
- Mutes
- Care of Instruments

Strings

- Violin, Viola, Cello, Double Bass (String Bass)
- Instrument construction
  Bridge
  Finger Board
  Scroll
- Bow construction
  Frog
  Tip
  Balance Point
  Horsehair
- Bowing techniques
  Down/Up
  Detache
  Pizzicato
  Col legno
  Legato
  Care of Instruments (Rosin for bow)

Conducting

- Stance
- Use of the Baton
- Grip
- Preparatory Beat/Downbeat
- Cueing and Use of Left Hand
- Ictus/Tactus
- Conducting Patterns
- Podium Etiquette
- Score Analysis
- Asymmetrical/Changing Meters
- Divided Beat Patterns (Subdivision)
- Instrumental Techniques
- Choral Techniques

Elementary Developmental Musical Expectations
Domain V: Music Education

Early Childhood and Kindergarten (Ages 3-5)*

- Limited vocal ranges
- Basic rhythmic responses (gross motor movement, steady beat, long/short)
- Sense of pitch often undeveloped
- Melodies performed alone or with a simple accompaniment (high/low, up/down/same concepts)
- Formal structures involve same and different melodic and rhythmic patterns and use of repetition as a unifying device
- Music concepts explored are loud or soft (dynamics) and fast or slow (tempo)

Primary Level (Grades 1-3; Ages 6-8)*

- Voices light in quality with a variety of ranges
- Simultaneous movements possible in rhythmic response
- Understands beat groupings in twos and threes
- Understands conjunct and disjunct melodic motion
- Formal structure adds the concept of phrases
- Understands that voices and instruments have distinctive sounds (timbre)
- Harmonic awareness develops

Intermediate Level (Grades 4-5; Ages 9-11)*

- Vocal mechanism developing rapidly (cambiata)
- Greater control of voice and breathing
- Improved coordination makes more complex rhythmic responses possible
- Improved fine motor coordination allows for beginning instrument instruction
- Understands symmetrical and asymmetrical meters
- Understands the concepts of melodic contour, major/minor/modal tonalities
- Formal structures typically include call and response, twelve bar blues, binary, ternary, rondo, and theme and variations
- Instruments identified by timbres and materials
- Musical elements identified and compared throughout music history
- Harmonic sense improves rapidly (improvises accompaniments on pitched and non-pitched classroom instruments; creates descants, introductions, and codas)

Grade levels and ages are approximate and may vary.

References by Domain

DOMAIN I: LISTENING

Anderson, W. M., and Campbell, P. S. (Compilers). Music Resources for Multicultural Perspectives. (2 compact discs). Music Educators National Conference, 1998.

Anderson, W. M., and Moore, M. C. (Compilers). Making Connections: Multicultural Music and the National Standards. (1 compact disc). Music Educators National Conference, 1998.

Burns, K.; Berkowitz, S.; Botstein, S.; Cuscuna, M.; Miller, P.; Novick, L.; Olds-Neal, N.; and Young, B. (Compilers). Ken Burn's Jazz: The Story of America's Music. (5 compact discs). Sony Music Entertainment Inc., 2000.

Crawford, R. (Compiler). Recordings for an Introduction to America's Music. (3 compact discs). Sony Music Entertainment Inc., 2001.

Hast; Cowdery; and Scott. Exploring the World of Music Telecourse Textbook/Reader/CD Package. Dubuque, IA: Kendall/Hunt Publishing, 1999.

Hill, W. L., and Griffin, C. (Compilers). The Instrumental History of Jazz. (2 compact discs). N2K Encoded Jazz, 1997.

Palisca, Claude, ed. The Norton Anthology of Western Music. 4th ed., Vol. I: Ancient to Baroque. New York: W. W. Norton, 2001.

Palisca, Claude, ed. The Norton Anthology of Western Music. 4th ed., Vol. II: Classic to Modern. New York: W. W. Norton, 2001.

Norton Recorded Anthology of Western Music: Volume I. (6 compact discs). Sony Music Entertainment Inc., 1996.

Norton Recorded Anthology of Western Music: Volume II. (6 compact discs). Sony Music Entertainment Inc., 1996.

The Norton Recordings Volume I: Gregorian Chant to Beethoven. (4 compact discs). Sony Music Entertainment Inc., 1999.

The Norton Recordings Volume II: Schubert to the Present. (4 compact discs). Sony Music Entertainment Inc., 1999.

DOMAIN II: MUSIC THEORY AND COMPOSITION

Adler, Samuel. The Study of Orchestration. 2nd ed. New York: W. W. Norton & Co., 1989.

References by Domain, cont'd.

Adler, Samuel. Workbook for The Study of Orchestration. 2nd ed. New York: W. W. Norton & Co., 1989.

Benjamin, Thomas; Horvit, Michael; and Nelson, Robert. Techniques and Materials of Tonal Music from the Common Practice Period Through the Twentieth Century. 6th ed. New York, NY: Schirmer Books, 2003.

Benward, Bruce, and White, Gary. Music in Theory and Practice. Vol. I, 6th ed. Madison, WI: Brown & Benchmark Publishers, 1997.

Kostka, Stefan, and Payne, Dorothy. Tonal Harmony. New York: McGraw-Hill Book Co., 2000.

Kostka, Stefan. Materials and Techniques of Twentieth-Century Music. 2nd ed. Englewood Cliffs, NJ: Prentice-Hall, Inc., 1999.

Ottman, Robert W. Elementary Harmony Theory and Practice. 5th ed. Englewood Cliffs, NJ: Prentice-Hall, Inc., 1998.

Ottman. Robert W. Advanced Harmony Theory and Practice. 4th ed. Englewood Cliffs, NJ: Prentice-Hall, Inc., 1992.

Steinke, Greg. Bridge to Twentieth-Century Music. Rev. ed. Boston, MA: Allyn & Bacon, 1999.

DOMAIN III: MUSIC HISTORY AND CULTURE

Amati-Campery, Alexandra, and Harker, Mara. History of Western Music in Outlines and Tables. Needham Heights, MA: Simon and Schuster Custom Pub., 1998.

Crawford, Richard. An Introduction to America's Music. New York, NY: W. W. Norton, 2001.

Ferrin, Jean. America's Musical Landscape. New York, NY: McGraw-Hill Book Co., 2002.

Grout, Donald, and Paliska, Claude. A History of Western Music. 6th ed. New York: W. W. Norton, 2001.

Hanning, Barbara R. Concise History of Western Music. 2nd ed. New York: W. W. Norton, 2002.

Hitchcock, H. Wiley. Music in the United States. 4th ed. Englewood Cliffs, NJ: Prentice Hall, 1998.

Kerman, Joseph. Listen. New York: Worth Publishers, 1996.

Appendix II
Resources and References

References by Domain, cont'd.

Kingman, Daniel. American Music: A Panorama. 3rd ed. New York: Schirmer Books/ Thomson Learning, 1998.

May, Elizabeth, ed. Music of Many Cultures: An Introduction. Berkeley, CA: University of California Press, 1980.

Miller, Hugh M. and Cockrell, Dale. History of Western Music. Harper Collins College Outline, 1991. (ISBN: 0064671070)

Nettl, Bruno, et al. Excursions in World Music. 3rd ed. Upper Saddle River, NJ: Prentice Hall, 2001.

Shelemay, Kay Kaufman. Soundscapes (Exploring Music in a Changing World). New York, NY: W. W. Norton, 2001.

Starr, Larry, and Waterman, Christopher. American Popular Music. New York, NY: Oxford University Press, 2003.

Titon, Jeff Todd, ed. Worlds of Music: An Introduction to the Music of the World's Peoples. 4th ed. Belmont, CA: Schirmer Books/Thompson Learning, 2002.

Wold, Milo; Martin, Gary; Miller, James; and Cykler, Edmund. An Outline History of Western Music. 9th ed. New York: McGraw-Hill Companies, Inc., 1998.

DOMAIN IV: MUSIC CLASSROOM PERFORMANCE

Barrier, Julie; Hansford, Jim; and Johnson, Mark. The Instrumental Resource. Nashville, TN: Church Street Press, 2002.

Bergonzi, Louis; Straub, Dorothy; and Witt, Anne. Strategies for Teaching Strings and Orchestra. Reston, VA: Music Educators National Conference, 1996.

Brinson, Barbara A. Choral Music Methods and Materials. New York, My: Schirmer Books, 1996.

Caldwell, Robert and Wall, Joan. Excellence in Singing: Multilevel Teaching & Multilevel Learning. (5 volume set). Dallas, TX: Caldwell Publishing Co., 2001.

Demorest, Steven M. Building Choral Excellence: Teaching SightSinging in the Choral Rehearsal. New York, NY: Oxford University Press, 2001.

Ericksen, Connie. Band Director's Curriculum Resource. West Nyack, NY: Parker Publishing Co., 1998.

References by Domain, cont'd.

Garretson, Robert L. Conducting Choral Music. 8th ed. Upper Saddle River, NJ: Prentice-Hall, Inc., 1998.

Gillespie, Robert, and Hamann, Donald. Strategies for Teaching Strings: Building a Successful String and Orchestra Program. New York, NY: Oxford University Press, 2004.

McKinney, James. The Diagnosis and Correction of Vocal Faults: A Manual for Teachers of Singing and for Choir Directors. Nashville, TN: Genevox Music Group, 1994.

DOMAIN V: MUSIC EDUCATION

Abeles, Harold; Hoffer, Charles; and Klotman, Robert. Foundations of Music Education. New York, NY: Schirmer Books, 1984.

Hackett, Patricia, and Lindeman, Carolynn. The Musical Classroom. 4th ed. Upper Saddle River, NJ: Prentice-Hall, Inc., 1997.

Hoffer, Charles. Teaching Music in the Secondary Schools. 4th ed. Belmont, CA: Wadsworth Publishing Co., 1991.

Mark, Michael. Contemporary Music Education. 2nd ed. New York, NY: Schirmer Books, 1986.

Mark, Michael, and Gary, Charles. A History of American Music Education. New York, NY: Schirmer Books, 1992.

Nye, Robert; Nye, Vernice; Martin, Gary; and, Van Rysselberghe, Mary Lou. Music in the Elementary School. 6th ed. Englewood Cliffs, NJ: Prentice-Hall, Inc., 1992.

Roach, Donald. Complete Secondary Choral Music Guide. West Nyack, NY: Parker Publishing Co., 1989.

Shehan-Campbell, Patricia. Lessons from the World. New York, NY: Schirmer Books, 1991.

Shehan-Campbell, Patricia, and Scott-Kassner, Carol. Music in Childhood. 2nd ed. New York, NY: Schirmer Books, 2002.

NOTE: The ETS/SBEC recommends several resources in the back of their study manual.

Resources

TExES Exam Contact Information:

For questions concerning all aspects of the TExES exams, including obtaining TExES Preparation Manuals, test dates, registration deadlines, admission, and scores contact:

> Educational Testing Service TExES Website:
> http://www.texes.ets.org
> 1-800-205-2626

The State Board of Educator Certification contact Information:

> SBEC Office of Accountability
> SBECPublicComment@tea.texas.gov
> www.tea.state.tx.us
> (512) 936-9831

Additional Study Resources:

(NOTE: Additional preparation resources listed in Section V of the ETS/SBEC TExES manual.)

- Additional books for various TExES exams on Amazon.com and in bookstores.

Additional Contacts:

- Texas Education Agency, 1701 North Congress Ave., Austin, TX 78701-1494, (512) 463-9734, FAX 512-463-9838

- Texas State Teachers Association, 316 West 12th Street, Austin, TX 78701 1-877-ASK-TSTA or 512-476-5355 http://www.tsta.org

- Secretary of State's Office: http://www.sos.state.tx.us

- Texas Center for Education Technology:
  http://www.tcet.unt.edu/home
  e-mail: tcetinfo@www.tcet.unt.edu

Resources

- TeachersNet: http://www.teachers.net

- The Association of Texas Professional Educators: http://www.atpe.org

- Texas Classroom Teachers Association: http://www.tcta.org

- Dept. of Education in Washington D.C.: http://www.ed.gov

- Pass the TExES Book and Seminar Program from Ed Publishing and Consulting
  http://www.passthetexes.com
  e-mail: edpublishing@passthetexes.com
  888-978-1922
  (Books ship from Dallas.)

Online Study Music Resources:

(NOTE: Additional preparation resources listed in Section V of the NES/SBEC TExES Music manual.)

- Music Educators National Conference (MENC) www.menc.org (see publications)
- Texas Music Educators Association (TMEA) www.tmea.org
- University Interscholastic League (UIL) www.uil.utexas.edu
- Center for Educator Development in the Fine Arts (CEDFA) http://finearts.esc20.net
- A History of Music Online Tutor www.wwnorton.com/grout/index.htm
  Contains chapter quizzes, chapter outlines, and interactive listening activities
- Kodaly and Orff Information www.wguc.org/cfk/teachers/training/rchart.asp
- Orchestra Seating Chart by Historical Period www.dsokids.com/seatingchart/index/html
- MacGAMUT 2003 (Ear Training and Dictation) www.macgamut.com
- Auralia (Ear Training and Aural Tests) www.sibelius.com/products/auralia
- Musition (Music Theory) www.sibelius.com/products/musition
- Sibelius Instruments (Guide to Band and Orchestral Instruments)
  www.sibelius.com/products/instruments

Appendix III

Seminar Packet/Practice Test

Appendix III

Pass the Texes Music

Seminar Packet/
Practice Test

Copyright © 2015 Ed Publishing

Competency Definitions

Domain I

1. **Elements**

   Competency 1:
   The teacher applies standard terminology to describe and analyze various elements in a musical recording.

2. **Styles and Genres**

   Competency 2:
   The teacher recognizes and describes music of diverse genres, styles, and cultures in a musical recording.

3. **Evaluation**

   Competency 3:
   The teacher evaluates and critiques musical compositions and performances in a musical recording.

Domain II

4. **Notation**

   Competency 4:
   The teacher knows how to read, write, and interpret standard music notation.

5. **Composition**

   Competency 5:
   The teacher understands methods and techniques of musical composition and improvisation and knows how to arrange music for specific purposes and settings.

Domain III

6. **Western Music**

   Competency 6:
   The teacher demonstrates a comprehensive knowledge of the history of Western music.

7. **Culture and Music**

   Competency 7:
   The teacher understands music of diverse genres, styles, and cultures and knows how music can reflect elements of a specific society or culture.

Domain IV

8. **Vocal Performance**

   Competency 8:
   The teacher demonstrates knowledge of methods and techniques for singing.

9. **Instrumental Performance**

   Competency 9:
   The teacher demonstrates knowledge of methods and techniques for playing musicalinstruments.

10. **Conducting**

    Competency 10:
    The teacher knows how to conduct vocal and instrumental performances.

Domain V

11. **Instruction (Planning and Implementing)**

    Competency 11:
    The teacher knows how to plan and implement effective music instruction.

12. **Learning Experiences in Music**

    Competency 12:
    The teacher knows how to provide students with learning experiences that enhance their musical knowledge, skills, and appreciation.

Worksheet 1
Building the Acronym

List the first letter of each Key Title for each Competency. Study them on the Competency study pages in this manual, and then write them from memory here. The headings below are the Domain titles.

I.   Listening
      1. _____
      2. _____
      3. _____

II.   Music Theory and Composition
      4. _____
      5. _____

III.   Music History and Culture
      6. _____
      7. _____

IV.   Music Classroom Performance
      8. _____
      9. _____
      10. _____

V.   Music Education
      11. _____
      12. _____

Appendix III

Worksheet 2
Competency Key Titles

List the Key Title for each Competency. Study them on the Competency study pages in this manual, and then write them from memory here.

I.   Listening
      1. _____
      2. _____
      3. _____

II. Music Theory and Composition
      4. _____
      5. _____

III. Music History and Culture
      6. _____
      7. _____

IV. Music Classroom Performance
      8. _____
      9. _____
      10. _____

V.   Music Education
      11. _____
      12. _____

Worksheet 3
Competency Definitions

State each Competency definition in your own words. Use conversational language, like "When I am teaching, I..." You might even want to memorize these definitions in your wording instead of the SBEC definitions. You can use simpler wording, use additional words, etc. NOTE: Personalizing these definitions will help you understand them.

1. _____
_____
_____

2. _____
_____
_____

3. _____
_____
_____

4. _____
_____
_____

5. _____
_____
_____

6. _____
_____
_____

7. _____
_____
_____

8. _____
_____
_____

9. _____
_____
_____

10. _____
_____
_____

11. _____
_____
_____

12. _____
_____

Appendix III

Worksheet 4
Key Descriptors

See the Descriptor exercise starting on p. 14 and in each Competency section. Write down <u>your</u> Key Descriptor phrases for each Descriptive Statement under all Competency headings below. (Refer to the TExES ETS/SBEC manual for the bullet points under each Competency to create your Descriptor phrases.) On each Competency section below there is space for you to write your Key Descriptor phrases. Copy when complete and carry with you for additional study.

Competency 1

_____
_____
_____
_____
_____
_____
_____
_____
_____
_____
_____
_____
_____
_____
_____

Competency 2

_____
_____
_____
_____
_____
_____
_____
_____
_____
_____
_____
_____
_____
_____
_____

Competency 3

_____
_____
_____
_____
_____
_____
_____
_____
_____
_____
_____
_____
_____
_____
_____

Competency 4

_____
_____
_____
_____
_____
_____
_____
_____
_____
_____
_____
_____
_____
_____
_____

Competency 5

_____
_____
_____
_____
_____
_____
_____
_____
_____
_____
_____
_____
_____
_____
_____

Competency 6

_____
_____
_____
_____
_____
_____
_____
_____
_____
_____
_____
_____
_____
_____
_____

Worksheet 4
Key Descriptors, cont'd.

Competency 7

_____
_____
_____
_____
_____
_____
_____
_____
_____
_____
_____
_____
_____

Competency 8

_____
_____
_____
_____
_____
_____
_____
_____
_____
_____
_____
_____
_____

Competency 9

_____
_____
_____
_____
_____
_____
_____
_____
_____
_____
_____
_____
_____

Competency 10

_____
_____
_____
_____
_____
_____
_____
_____
_____
_____
_____
_____
_____

Competency 11

_____
_____
_____
_____
_____
_____
_____
_____
_____
_____
_____
_____
_____

Competency 12

_____
_____
_____
_____
_____
_____
_____
_____
_____
_____
_____
_____
_____

Appendix III

PRACTICE TEST WORKSHEET

1) Restate the question in your own words if necessary. _____
_____
_____

2) Determine what Competency the question is referring to. _____

3) State why you think this is the correct Competency. _____
_____
_____

4) Based on the competency you chose, state your answer _____

5) State why this answer is correct, and why it connects to the Competency you chose. _____
_____
_____

6) Look up the correct competency and answer in the Answer Key.

7) Analysis: What is the reason the test writers chose the answer they did (whether you were right or wrong)? This analysis will help you understand the SBEC point of view. _____
_____
_____

. . . .

1) Restate the question in your own words if necessary. _____
_____
_____

2) Determine what Competency the question is referring to. _____

3) State why you think this is the correct Competency. _____
_____
_____

4) Based on the competency you chose, state your answer _____

5) State why this answer is correct, and why it connects to the Competency you chose. _____
_____
_____

6) Look up the correct competency and answer in the Answer Key.

7) Analysis: What is the reason the test writers chose the answer they did (whether you were right or wrong)? This analysis will help you understand the SBEC point of view. _____
_____
_____

Practice Test Questions

Note: This sampling of questions is used for the purpose of illustrating our practice test method. Our 7-question worksheet documents your thought processes while answering questions. It is important to know why you are making certain choices, as well as do an analysis of the test writer's answers. You may copy the page at left several times, and use it as you answer other questions you might be using from another publishing company, your Education Service Center, ACP, university, school district, or other source.

LISTENING

(Questions 1-5 are shown here as examples of the types of listening questions on the actual TExES exam).

1. Who is the probable composer of this piece?

A. Debussy
B. Bartok
C. Schubert
D. Bach

2. Name the type of chord heard in this example.

A. Diminished
B. Minor
C. Augmented
D. Major

3. What is the probable style period of this piece?

A. Classical
B. 20th Century
C. Baroque
D. Romantic

4. Name the mode heard in this example.

A. Dorian
B. Ionian
C. Lydian
D. Phrygian

5. Who is the probable composer of this piece?

A. Josquin
B. Mozart
C. Bach
D. Chopin

6. Name the composer who used American music of all kinds, regions, and ages, including Shaker tunes, square dancing, jazz and orchestra pieces, and cowboy songs in ballets.

A. Aaron Copland
B. Samuel Barber
C. Charles Ives
D. Randall Thompson

1) Restate the question in your own words if necessary. _____
_____
_____

2) Determine what Competency the question is referring to. _____

3) State why you think this is the correct Competency. _____
_____
_____

4) Based on the competency you chose, state your answer _____

5) State why this answer is correct, and why it connects to the Competency you chose. _____
_____
_____

6) Look up the correct competency and answer in the Answer Key.

7) Analysis: What is the reason the test writers chose the answer they did (whether you were right or wrong)? This analysis will help you understand the SBEC point of view. _____
_____
_____

7. Storing a woodwind instrument without removing the inside moisture would most likely result in damage to which of the following parts?

A. Keys
B. Posts
C. Bell
D. Pads

1) Restate the question in your own words if necessary. _____
_____
_____

2) Determine what Competency the question is referring to. _____

3) State why you think this is the correct Competency. _____
_____
_____

4) Based on the competency you chose, state your answer _____

5) State why this answer is correct, and why it connects to the Competency you chose. _____
_____
_____

6) Look up the correct competency and answer in the Answer Key.

7) Analysis: What is the reason the test writers chose the answer they did (whether you were right or wrong)? This analysis will help you understand the SBEC point of view. _____
_____
_____

8. Which style of music developed in Kentucky and uses violin, mandolin, guitar, banjo, and solo vocals?

A. Country Western
B. Bluegrass
C. Jazz
D. Gospel

1) Restate the question in your own words if necessary. _____
_____
_____

2) Determine what Competency the question is referring to. _____

3) State why you think this is the correct Competency. _____
_____
_____

4) Based on the competency you chose, state your answer _____

5) State why this answer is correct, and why it connects to the Competency you chose. _____
_____
_____

6) Look up the correct competency and answer in the Answer Key.

7) Analysis: What is the reason the test writers chose the answer they did (whether you were right or wrong)? This analysis will help you understand the SBEC point of view. _____
_____
_____

9. Name the term for plucking the string on bowed string instruments.

A. Glissando
B. Staccato
C. Marcato
D. Pizzicato

1) Restate the question in your own words if necessary. _____
_____
_____

2) Determine what Competency the question is referring to. _____

3) State why you think this is the correct Competency. _____
_____
_____

4) Based on the competency you chose, state your answer _____

5) State why this answer is correct, and why it connects to the Competency you chose. _____
_____
_____

6) Look up the correct competency and answer in the Answer Key.

7) Analysis: What is the reason the test writers chose the answer they did (whether you were right or wrong)? This analysis will help you understand the SBEC point of view. _____
_____
_____

10. In teaching children to feel the beat with their whole body, what is the term used for clapping and slapping the thighs?

A. Eurhythmics
B. Solfege
C. Detache
D. Patschen

1) Restate the question in your own words if necessary. _____
_____
_____

2) Determine what Competency the question is referring to. _____

3) State why you think this is the correct Competency. _____
_____
_____

4) Based on the competency you chose, state your answer _____

5) State why this answer is correct, and why it connects to the Competency you chose. _____
_____
_____

6) Look up the correct competency and answer in the Answer Key.

7) Analysis: What is the reason the test writers chose the answer they did (whether you were right or wrong)? This analysis will help you understand the SBEC point of view. _____
_____
_____

11. Mr. Jones has just been hired as the band director at the local high school, and he is preparing to order music for the fall semester. Even though he is a first year teacher, he is not concerned about choosing music because he kept a list of repertoire that his college band played, looking forward to the time when he could direct these pieces with his own ensemble. Mr. Jones ordered some of the selections, did thorough preparation before the first rehearsal, and was

enthusiastic about introducing each piece to the band. When he met with less than positive results after several rehearsals, he realized he had chosen the music with little regard for:

A. the interest level of the students
B. the amount of available rehearsal time per week
C. the ability level and instrumentation of the band
D. the acoustical properties of the rehearsal hall

1) Restate the question in your own words if necessary. _____
_____
_____

2) Determine what Competency the question is referring to. _____

3) State why you think this is the correct Competency. _____
_____
_____

4) Based on the competency you chose, state your answer _____

5) State why this answer is correct, and why it connects to the Competency you chose. _____
_____
_____

6) Look up the correct competency and answer in the Answer Key.

7) Analysis: What is the reason the test writers chose the answer they did (whether you were right or wrong)? This analysis will help you understand the SBEC point of view. _____
_____
_____

12. In a plagal cadence, what precedes the final tonic chord?

A. Submediant
B. Subdominant
C. Dominant
D. Supertonic

1) Restate the question in your own words if necessary. _____
_____
_____
_

2) Determine what Competency the question is referring to. _____

3) State why you think this is the correct Competency. _____

4) *Based on the competency you chose, state your answer* _____

5) *State why this answer is correct, and why it connects to the Competency you chose.* _____

_____

6) *Look up the correct competency and answer in the Answer Key.*

7) *Analysis: What is the reason the test writers chose the answer they did (whether you were right or wrong)? This analysis will help you understand the SBEC point of view.* _____

_____

_____

13. Name the term for the fugal process of overlapping entrances of the subject in several voices simultaneously.

A. Augmentation
B. Diminution
C. Stretto
D. Sequence

1) *Restate the question in your own words if necessary.* _____

_____

_____

2) *Determine what Competency the question is referring to.* _____

3) *State why you think this is the correct Competency.* _____

_____

_____

4) *Based on the competency you chose, state your answer* _____

5) *State why this answer is correct, and why it connects to the Competency you chose.* _____

_____

_____

6) *Look up the correct competency and answer in the Answer Key.*

7) *Analysis: What is the reason the test writers chose the answer they did (whether you were right or wrong)? This analysis will help you understand the SBEC point of view.* _____

_____

_____

14. Which of the following assessment methods would a teacher use in evaluating a student's ability to interpret dynamic markings?

A. Personal Interview
B. Performance Observation
C. Cooperative Learning
D. Benchmark Testing

*Restate the question in your own words if necessary. _____
_____
_____

*Determine what competency the question is referring to. _____
*State why you think this is the correct Competency. _____
_____
_____

*Based on the Competency you chose, state your answer _____
*State why this answer connects to the Competency you chose. _____
_____
_____

*Look up the correct competency and answer in the answer key.

*Analysis: What is the reason the test writers chose the answer they did (whether you were right or wrong)? This analysis will help you understand the SBEC point of view._____
_____
_____

15. The spelling E, F#, G#, A#, B#, C##, E represents what type of scale?

A. Melodic minor
B. Chromatic
C. Harmonic minor
D. Whole tone

*Restate the question in your own words if necessary. _____
_____
_____

*Determine what competency the question is referring to. _____
*State why you think this is the correct Competency. _____
_____
_____

*Based on the Competency you chose, state your answer _____
*State why this answer connects to the Competency you chose. _____
_____
_____

*Look up the correct competency and answer in the answer key.

*Analysis: What is the reason the test writers chose the answer they did (whether you were right or wrong)? This analysis will help you understand the SBEC point of view._____
_____
_____

16. Which of these musical styles uses an orchestra of metal and bamboo xylophones, gongs, and drums to accompany dances and theatre pieces?
A. Indian raga

B. Chinese folk music
C. Spanish flamenco
D. Indonesian gamelan

1) Restate the question in your own words if necessary. _____
_____
_____

2) Determine what Competency the question is referring to. _____

3) State why you think this is the correct Competency. _____
_____
_____

4) Based on the competency you chose, state your answer _____

5) State why this answer is correct, and why it connects to the Competency you chose. _____
_____
_____

6) Look up the correct competency and answer in the Answer Key.

7) Analysis: What is the reason the test writers chose the answer they did (whether you were right or wrong)? This analysis will help you understand the SBEC point of view. _____
_____
_____

17. One of Ms. Smith's ensembles is the 9th and 10th grade women's chorus which serves as a training choir for beginning singers. After voice checks with each student, she notices that many of the girls sing primarily in chest voice and seem to have little experience with head voice tone production. What types of vocal exercises would be best for achieving optimum head voice tone quality?

A. Ascending patterns
B. Fast scale patterns
C. Descending patterns
D. Long sustained patterns

1) Restate the question in your own words if necessary. _____
_____
_____

2) Determine what Competency the question is referring to. _____

3) State why you think this is the correct Competency. _____
_____
_____

4) Based on the competency you chose, state your answer _____

5) State why this answer is correct, and why it connects to the Competency you chose. _____
_____
_____

6) Look up the correct competency and answer in the Answer Key.

7) Analysis: What is the reason the test writers chose the answer they did (whether you were right or wrong)? This analysis will help you understand the SBEC point of view. _____

_____

_____

18. Which of the following is not a property of snare drum design?

A. Shell
B. Head
C. Foot pedals
D. Tension rods

1) Restate the question in your own words if necessary. _____

_____

_____

2) Determine what Competency the question is referring to. _____

3) State why you think this is the correct Competency. _____

_____

_____

4) Based on the competency you chose, state your answer _____

5) State why this answer is correct, and why it connects to the Competency you chose. _____

_____

_____

6) Look up the correct competency and answer in the Answer Key.

7) Analysis: What is the reason the test writers chose the answer they did (whether you were right or wrong)? This analysis will help you understand the SBEC point of view. _____

_____

_____

19. What is the instrumentation of a string quartet?

A. violin, viola, cello, bass
B. violin, violin, viola, cello
C. violin, violin, cello, bass
D. violin, viola cello, piano

1) Restate the question in your own words if necessary. _____

_____

_____

2) Determine what Competency the question is referring to. _____

3) State why you think this is the correct Competency. _____

_____

_____

4) Based on the competency you chose, state your answer _____

5) State why this answer is correct, and why it connects to the Competency you chose. _____

_____

_____

6) Look up the correct competency and answer in the Answer Key.

7) Analysis: What is the reason the test writers chose the answer they did (whether you were right or wrong)? This analysis will help you understand the SBEC point of view. _____

_____

_____

20. The left hand is not usually used for which of the following in conducting?

A. Cueing entrances
B. Dynamic and tempo changes
C. Starting and stopping the ensemble
D. Mirroring the beat pattern of the right hand

1) Restate the question in your own words if necessary. _____

_____

_____

2) Determine what Competency the question is referring to. _____

3) State why you think this is the correct Competency. _____

_____

_____

4) Based on the competency you chose, state your answer _____

5) State why this answer is correct, and why it connects to the Competency you chose. _____

_____

_____

6) Look up the correct competency and answer in the Answer Key.

7) Analysis: What is the reason the test writers chose the answer they did (whether you were right or wrong)? This analysis will help you understand the SBEC point of view. _____

_____

_____

21. Since the late 1980s, schools have integrated handicapped students into the regular classroom, as well as special classes such as music, art, and physical education, using a model called:
A. Collaboration
B. Multimodality
C. Self-contained
D. Inclusion

1) Restate the question in your own words if necessary. _____
_____
_____

2) Determine what Competency the question is referring to. _____

3) State why you think this is the correct Competency. _____
_____
_____

4) Based on the competency you chose, state your answer _____

5) State why this answer is correct, and why it connects to the Competency you chose. _____
_____
_____

6) Look up the correct competency and answer in the Answer Key.

7) Analysis: What is the reason the test writers chose the answer they did (whether you were right or wrong)? This analysis will help you understand the SBEC point of view. _____
_____
_____

22. Ms. Morales is challenged by off-task behavior in her 5th grade music class during large-group instruction. Her greatest responsibility in solving this classroom management issue is to:

A. plan focused lessons with appropriate pacing
B. allow students to choose from several small-group activities
C. assign students individual study packets
D. enlist help from the classroom teacher in observing the music class

1) Restate the question in your own words if necessary. _____
_____
_____

2) Determine what Competency the question is referring to. _____

3) State why you think this is the correct Competency. _____
_____
_____

4) Based on the competency you chose, state your answer _____

5) State why this answer is correct, and why it connects to the Competency you chose. _____
_____
_____

6) Look up the correct competency and answer in the Answer Key.

7) Analysis: What is the reason the test writers chose the answer they did (whether you were right or wrong)? This analysis will help you understand the SBEC point of view. _____
_____
_____

Answer Key

Questions 1-5 represent Domain I: Listening. They are shown in the practice test to indicate types of multiple choice listening questions that may be found on the TExES exam. Because of the nature of this material, there are no recorded examples on the practice test.

1. Domain I: Listening
2. Domain I: Listening
3. Domain I: Listening
4. Domain I: Listening
5. Domain I: Listening
6. A   Competency 006
7. D   Competency 009
8. B   Competency 007
9. D   Competency 009
10. D   Competency 011
11. C   Competency 011
12. B   Competency 004
13. C   Competency 005
14. B   Competency 011
15. D   Competency 004
16. D   Competency 007
17. C   Competency 008
18. C   Competency 009
19. B   Competency 009
20. D   Competency 010
21. D   Competency 011
22. A   Competency 012
23. B   Competency 006
24. B   Competency 012
25. C   Competency 012

NES/SBEC
Competencies and Descriptive Statements

Starting on the next page are the bulleted Competency Descriptive Statements for this test from the ETS/SBEC manual. The material is directly from the official manual so the page numbers will not correspond with the page numbers in our book. We have included this portion of the manual so that you can do the "Descriptor Exercise" explained in the "Steps for Success" on p. 10. The PDF-formatted preparation manual may be downloaded from the ETS/SBEC website, and it is also enclosed in the supplementary files with this manual. You must use Acrobat Reader® to open the file.

Domains and Competencies

The content covered by this test is organized into broad areas of content called **domains**. Each domain covers one or more of the educator standards for this field. Within each domain, the content is further defined by a set of **competencies**. Each competency is composed of two major parts:

- The **competency statement**, which broadly defines what an entry-level educator in this field in Texas public schools should know and be able to do.
- The **descriptive statements**, which describe in greater detail the knowledge and skills eligible for testing.

Domain I — Listening

Competency 001: *The teacher applies standard terminology to describe and analyze various elements in a musical recording.*

The beginning teacher:

A. Interprets music symbols and terms aurally (e.g., dynamics, embellishments, articulation, tempo markings), identifies specific melodic and harmonic intervals and recognizes scales and pitch collections (e.g., modal, major, minor, pentatonic, whole-tone).

B. Identifies different rhythms and meters and interprets rhythmic and melodic phrases aurally (e.g., syncopation, hemiola, augmentation, contour, sequence, repetition).

C. Recognizes and describes the melody, harmony and texture of a musical work (e.g., modal, tonal, atonal, ostinato, doublings, melody and countermelody).

D. Analyzes chordal structures (e.g., major, minor, dominant seventh, diminished seventh), harmonic progressions, cadences (e.g., authentic, half, deceptive, plagal) and harmonic textures (e.g., polyphonic, homophonic, monophonic).

Competency 002: *The teacher recognizes and describes music of diverse genres, styles and cultures in a musical recording.*

The beginning teacher:

A. Recognizes and demonstrates knowledge of major periods, styles and individuals in the history of music and their significance (e.g., Middle Ages, Renaissance, Baroque, Classical, Romantic, Modern).

B. Characterizes and classifies examples of non-Western music (e.g., Indonesian gamelan, African drumming, Indian raga, Cuban salsa) by genre, style, culture or historical period.

NOTE: After clicking on a link, right click and select "Previous View" to go back to original text.

C. Recognizes and describes music that reflects the heritage of the United States and Texas (e.g., folk songs, work songs, jazz, blues, gospel, Tejano, country, bluegrass).

Competency 003: *The teacher evaluates and critiques musical compositions and performances in a musical recording.*

The beginning teacher:

A. Identifies vocal and instrumental sounds and distinguishes among timbres (e.g., voice and instrument types and ensembles).

B. Recognizes accurate pitch, intonation, rhythm and characteristic tone quality; recognizes and diagnoses performance problems; and detects errors accurately.

C. Identifies and analyzes musical forms in performance and listening repertoire (e.g., twelve-bar blues, binary, ternary) and characteristics of style and expression in musical performance (e.g., dynamics, tempo, articulation, embellishments).

Domain II — Music Theory and Composition

Competency 004: *The teacher knows how to read, write and interpret standard music notation.*

The beginning teacher:

A. Knows standard music terminology and identifies and interprets music symbols and terms from notation (e.g., dynamics, embellishments, articulation markings, tempo markings).

B. Recognizes clefs, keys and meters; recognizes scales and pitch collections (e.g., modal, major, minor, pentatonic, whole-tone); identifies specific melodic and harmonic intervals; and identifies different rhythms and meters.

C. Reads melodies in various modes and tonalities; interprets rhythmic and melodic phrases from notation; and reads music that incorporates complex rhythmic patterns in simple, compound and asymmetric meters.

D. Recognizes and describes melody, harmony and texture of a musical work (e.g., modal, tonal, atonal, ostinato, doublings, melody and countermelody).

E. Analyzes chordal structures (e.g., major, minor, dominant seventh, diminished seventh), harmonic progressions, cadences (e.g., authentic, half, deceptive, plagal) and harmonic textures (e.g., polyphonic, homophonic, monophonic).

NOTE: After clicking on a link, right click and select "Previous View" to go back to original text.

Competency 005: *The teacher understands methods and techniques of musical composition and improvisation and knows how to arrange music for specific purposes and settings.*

The beginning teacher:

A. Knows how to compose and arrange simple vocal and instrumental music for specific purposes and settings (e.g., scoring techniques, transpositions, ranges).

B. Analyzes compositional devices (e.g., repetition/contrast, delayed resolution, augmentation/diminution, fugue, tone row, ostinato) and applies knowledge of music forms (e.g., binary, ternary, rondo, concerto, opera, twelve-bar blues).

C. Knows how to improvise melodically, rhythmically and harmonically (e.g., question and answer, variation, twelve-bar blues).

D. Applies criteria for evaluating and critiquing musical compositions, evaluates specific musical works and styles using appropriate music terminology and knows how to offer constructive suggestions for the improvement of a musical composition.

Domain III — Music History and Culture

Competency 006: *The teacher demonstrates a comprehensive knowledge of the history of Western music.*

The beginning teacher:

A. Recognizes and describes major periods (e.g., Middle Ages, Renaissance, Baroque, Classical, Romantic, Modern), styles and individuals in the history of Western music and their significance.

B. Characterizes and classifies examples of Western music by genre, style, culture or historical period.

Competency 007: *The teacher understands music of diverse genres, styles and cultures and knows how music can reflect elements of a specific society or culture.*

The beginning teacher:

A. Characterizes and classifies examples of non-Western music (e.g., Indonesian gamelan, African drumming, Indian raga, Cuban salsa) by genre, style, culture or historical period.

B. Recognizes and describes music that reflects the heritage of the United States and Texas (e.g., folk songs, work songs, jazz, blues, gospel, Tejano, country, bluegrass).

NOTE: After clicking on a link, right click and select "Previous View" to go back to original text.

C. Analyzes the purposes and roles of music in society and culture and analyzes relationships between music and society, culture and technology.

Domain IV — Music Classroom Performance

Competency 008: *The teacher demonstrates knowledge of methods and techniques for singing.*

The beginning teacher:

A. Understands performance skills and appropriate techniques for singing (e.g., tone production, sight-singing methods).

B. Understands proper health techniques to use during vocal rehearsals and performances (e.g., maintaining good posture, protecting the changing voice).

C. Selects appropriate vocal literature to enhance technical skills and provide musical challenges.

D. Understands standard terminology used in communicating about students' musical skills and performances.

E. Knows how to offer meaningful prescriptions for correcting performance problems and errors (e.g., diction, tone production, intonation, phrasing) and understands the constructive use of criticism when evaluating musical skills or performances.

Competency 009: *The teacher demonstrates knowledge of methods and techniques for playing musical instruments.*

The beginning teacher:

A. Understands performance skills and appropriate playing techniques (e.g., bowing, fingering, embouchure, rudiments) for a range of instruments (e.g., band, orchestral, classroom).

B. Understands proper health techniques to use during instrumental rehearsals and performances (e.g., posture, hand position, instrument maintenance).

C. Selects appropriate instrumental literature to enhance technical skills and provide musical challenges.

D. Understands standard terminology used in communicating about students' musical skills and performances.

E. Knows how to offer meaningful prescriptions for correcting performance problems and errors (e.g., intonation, vibrato, articulation, tone production) and understands the constructive use of criticism when evaluating musical skills or performances.

NOTE: After clicking on a link, right click and select "Previous View" to go back to original text.

Competency 010: *The teacher knows how to conduct vocal and instrumental performances.*

The beginning teacher:

A. Selects appropriate conducting techniques for small and large ensembles (e.g., basic conducting patterns, techniques for communicating expression markings, cuing techniques).

B. Demonstrates knowledge of appropriate vocal and instrumental performance techniques for small and large ensembles.

C. Knows how to interpret music through performance and demonstrates knowledge of musical performance styles.

D. Demonstrates knowledge of a varied musical repertoire for vocal and instrumental performance.

E. Understands legal and ethical issues related to the use or performance of music in an educational setting, applies knowledge of copyright laws to make appropriate decisions about the use of music in an educational setting and knows federal and state policies and regulations concerning the use and performance of music.

Domain V — Music Education

Competency 011: *The teacher knows how to plan and implement effective music instruction.*

The beginning teacher:

A. Demonstrates knowledge of the content and performance standards for music that comprise the Texas Essential Knowledge and Skills (TEKS) and recognizes the significance of the TEKS in developing a music curriculum.

B. Knows how to use multiple forms of assessment and knowledge of the TEKS to help determine students' progress in developing music skills and understanding, applies knowledge of techniques and criteria for ongoing assessment of students' musical knowledge and skills and knows how to use assessment results to help develop instructional plans.

C. Demonstrates an understanding of appropriate sequencing of music instruction and knows how to deliver developmentally appropriate music instruction that is sequenced and delivered in ways that encourage active engagement in learning and make instructional content meaningful.

D. Knows how to adapt instructional methods to provide appropriate learning experiences for students with varied needs, learning modalities and levels of development and musical experience.

NOTE: After clicking on a link, right click and select "Previous View" to go back to original text.

E. Knows how to provide instruction that promotes students' understanding and application of fundamental principles of music and that offers students varied opportunities to make music using instruments and voice, to respond to a wide range of musical styles and genres and to evaluate music of various types.

F. Demonstrates an understanding of materials and resources available for use in music education and applies knowledge of procedures and criteria for selecting an appropriate repertoire for the music class.

G. Knows how to use varied materials, resources and technologies to promote students' creativity, learning and performance and understands the use of technology as a tool in the music class.

H. Instructs students to apply skills for forming and communicating critical judgments about music and music performance; knows strategies and benefits of promoting students' critical-thinking and problem-solving skills in relation to music; and knows how to provide students with frequent opportunities to use critical-thinking and problem-solving skills in analyzing, creating and responding to music.

Competency 012: *The teacher knows how to provide students with learning experiences that enhance their musical knowledge, skills and appreciation.*

The beginning teacher:

A. Demonstrates awareness of the importance of helping students develop music skills that are relevant to their own lives and of providing students with a level of musical self-sufficiency that encourages lifelong enjoyment of music.

B. Knows how to provide students with opportunities to contribute to the music class by drawing on their personal experiences and by encouraging students to pursue musical knowledge independently.

C. Demonstrates knowledge of various music and music-related career options and knows how to promote music as an integral element in students' lives, whether as a vocation or as an avocation.

D. Knows how to help students develop an understanding and appreciation of various cultures through music instruction and discussion of current events related to music and knows how to incorporate a diverse musical repertoire into instruction, including music from both Western and non-Western traditions.

E. Knows how to integrate music instruction with other subject areas and analyzes relationships among the content, concepts and processes of music, the other fine arts and other subjects.

NOTE: After clicking on a link, right click and select "Previous View" to go back to original text.

F. Applies strategies and procedures for effectively managing and organizing the music class in various settings (e.g., rehearsal room, concert hall, marching field); knows how to manage time, instructional resources and physical space effectively for the music class; and knows how to teach students concert etiquette.

G. Demonstrates knowledge of techniques for effectively and efficiently managing varied resources for the music education program and applies strategies for managing and documenting the use and condition of musical instruments and other materials in the music program.

NOTE: After clicking on a link, right click and select "Previous View" to go back to original text.

Pass the TEXES Test Prep Program
Directions for Using the Study Module CD

Included with the supplementary files is our interactive PowerPoint® study module. The module will help you understand the framework of the Music Competencies. See directions below regarding opening and using this module. Also included is the ETS/SBEC Study Manual in PDF format. You may open this with Acrobat Reader®, a program you should already have on your computer. Simply do a search for "Acrobat Reader", open "Acrobat Reader" and then open the study manual.

NOTE: The files are locked to protect the copyrighted contents. You may get a message about "read-only." Simply click "OK." ALSO, IF YOU WANT TO STOP THE MODULE AT ANY POINT PRESS THE "ESC" KEY ON YOUR KEYBOARD. **ENJOY THE MODULE!**

PC USERS

A. If you have PowerPoint® follow these directions:

1. Insert the CD. Go to the CD drive. Double click on the file "TEXES Music Show.pps " or "TExES Music Module.ppt".

2. You may get a message stating that you are opening a Macintosh file and the file will be translated. Click "OK."

3. Your module will then open and you must click your mouse to advance to the following page. If the module does not open in the "Show" mode, go under the menu title "Slide Show" and choose "View Show" mode. It is set up for manual advancing but may give you a choice—manual advancing is the mode you want. Once the show starts you are on your way! Follow the directions in the yellow box on each slide.

B. If you do not have PowerPoint® or if you cannot open the file, follow these directions:

1. You must use the enclosed VIEWER in the PC Viewer folder.

2. Click twice on the Viewer application called "PPView 97" and ending in ".exe". The application will install on your C drive. After installation go to Programs and choose the new PowerPoint® Viewer. The application will open and will ask you for the PowerPoint® file you want to open.

3. Choose the "Texes Music Show" or the "Texes Music Module.ppt" and the module will open. (If you do not see the list of files in the window go to "File Name" and type in "Texes Music Show" or "Texes Music Module"). Your module will then open and you must click your mouse to advance to the following page. If the module does not open in the "show" mode and fill your screen, go under the menu title "Slide Show" and choose "View" mode. It is set up for manual advancing but may give you a choice—manual advancing is want. Once the show starts you are on your way! Follow the directions in the yellow box on each slide.

MAC USERS

A. If you have PowerPoint® on the Mac follow these directions:

1. Launch PowerPoint® and open the document "Texes Music Show.pps" or "Texes Music Module.ppt" on the CD.

2. The module will then open and you must click your mouse to advance to the following page. If it does not open up as a "show" and fill your screen go under the "Slide Show" menu heading and choose "View Show" mode. It is set up for manual advancing but in case it gives you a choice, that is what you want. You will be clicking your mouse to advance to each slide. Once the show starts you are on your way! Follow the directions in the yellow box on each slide.

B. If you do not have PowerPoint® or have an older version than 4.0 follow these directions:

1. You must use PowerPoint® VIEWER which is downloadable from the Microsoft site. Please e-mail us at edpublishing@passthetexes.com and we will e-mail the long link to the correct Viewer to you. Then you can download it, install it, and open the file. Go to #2 once you get the Viewer open.

2. Click twice on the Viewer icon. A window comes up and asks you for the PowerPoint® file you want to open. Go to the CD.

3. Choose the "Texes Music Show.pps" or "Texes Music Module.ppt" and choose "show" and the module will open. You must click your mouse to advance to the following page. If it does not open up as a "show" and fill your screen go under the "Slide Show" menu heading and choose "View Show" mode. It is set up for manual advancing but in case it gives you a choice, that is what you want. You will be clicking your mouse to advance to each slide. Once the show starts you are on your way! Follow the directions in the yellow box on each slide.